A Brave, Active, and Intrepid Soldier

Lieutenant Colonel Richard Campbell of the Virginia Continental Line

Michael Cecere

HERITAGE BOOKS
2020

HERITAGE BOOKS
AN IMPRINT OF HERITAGE BOOKS, INC.

Books, CDs, and more—Worldwide

For our listing of thousands of titles see our website
at
www.HeritageBooks.com

Published 2020 by
HERITAGE BOOKS, INC.
Publishing Division
5810 Ruatan Street
Berwyn Heights, Md. 20740

Copyright © 2020 Michael Cecere

Cover: *The Battle of Eutaw Springs: The British centre breaking before the charge of the Virginia and Maryland regiments.*
Source note: The story of the Revolution. (New York: Scribner, 1903)
Lodge, Henry Cabot (1850–1924), author.
From
The New York Public Library
http://digitalcollections.nypl.org/items/510d47e0-f65c-a3d9-e040-e00a18064a99

All rights reserved. No part of this book may be reproduced or transmitted in any form or by any means, electronic or mechanical, including photocopying, recording or by any information storage and retrieval system without written permission from the author, except for the inclusion of brief quotations in a review.

International Standard Book Number
Paperbound: 978-0-7884-5908-5

Acknowledgements

As with all of my books, I'd like to thank my friends in the Revolutionary War reenacting hobby for the continued support and encouragement. I also want to thank the Rockefeller Library at Colonial Williamsburg, the research library at the Jamestown--Yorktown Foundation, and the Public Library of Shenandoah County. These wonderful facilities provided me with the resources necessary to write this book.

Contents

Ch. 1   "They are both Equally Alert, Zealous and Spirited." 1745-1776..........................1

Ch. 2   " I am Intent on Giving the Enemy Battle Wherever I Should Meet Them." 1777.........................19

Ch. 3   " [Major] Campbell Behaved Gallantly During the Action." 1777..........................37

Ch. 4   "To Chastise and Terrify the Savages, and to Check their Ravages on the Frontier." 1778-80..........................57

Ch. 5   "The Present Moment is Critical" 1780-81 73

Ch. 6   "He was the Great and the Firm Patriot." 1781..........................97

Bibliography..........................123

Index..........................133

Chapter One

They are both Equally Alert, Zealous and Spirited.

1745 – 1776

Richard Campbell is one of thousands of Revolutionary War veterans whose service and sacrifice in America's War for Independence is largely unknown to his countrymen today. Campbell answered the call to serve in early 1776 at age 31, leaving his wife Rebecca and five young sons in Woodstock, Virginia (in the Shenandoah Valley).[1] An attorney, undersheriff (deputy) and tavern keeper who kept several slaves and indentured servants, Campbell was not heavily involved in the political affairs that led to the war.[2] He held no elective office or served on any committees, although he did host the first meeting of the Dunmore County Committee at his home (and tavern) in Woodstock in January 1775. The eighteen "gentlemen" of the committee met at Campbell's home on the heels of their selection by the freeholders of Dunmore (now Shenandoah) County to implement the measures adopted by the First Continental Congress the previous fall.[3]

---

[1] Gaius M. Brumbaugh, "List of the Number of Persons in Dunmore County...Taken by Richard Campbell, November, 1775," *Revolutionary War Records,* Vol. 1, (Washington, D.C., 1936), 591 and Amelia C. Gilreath, *Order Book, 1772-1774, Shenandoah County, VA,* Abstracted, (1986), 3 and Val McAlister, *The Campbell's*: *Genealogy and History,* (unpublished), 80-81

[2] Gilreath, 2, 6, 7, 15, 27, 140, and Brumbaugh, 591 and McAlister, 80

[3] William J. Van Schreeven and Robert L. Scribner, eds., "Dunmore County Committee, January 10, 1775," *Revolutionary Virginia : The Road to Independence,* Vol. 2, (University Press of Virginia, 1975), 229

Although Richard Campbell did not play a leading role in opposing British policies prior to the Revolutionary War, he did command a company of militia in Dunmore County before the war erupted.[4] His appointment was probably connected to his position as undersheriff in the county as well as the respect many residents of Dunmore County held for him as one of the few attorneys in the county.

Campbell's leadership in the county militia prior to 1776 likely earned him a commission early that year from the Dunmore County committee as captain of a company of Virginia regulars in Colonel Peter Muhlenberg's 8th Virginia Regiment.[5] This regiment, one of six new regiments authorized by the 4th Virginia Convention in late 1775, quadrupled Virginia's regular forces and signified Virginia's determination to fight the British.

Colonel Muhlenberg's soldiers were all recruited from the frontier counties of Virginia for two years of service. They carried rifles instead of smoothbore muskets and were referred to as the German Regiment by the Fourth Virginia Convention because of the large number of Germans from the Shenandoah Valley that the regiment was expected to raise.[6]

---

[4] Brumbaugh, "Military Districts, Old Dunmore County, Virginia," *Revolutionary War Records,* Vol. 1, 601

[5] Robert L. Scribner and Brent Tarter, eds., "Accot. of the Regular Officers of this [Dunmore] County, January 23, 1776," *Revolutionary Virginia: The Road to Independence*, Vol. 6, (Univ. Press of Virginia, 1981), 19

[6] Frank E. Grizzard, ed., "Colonel Muhlenberg to General Washington, February 23, 1777," *The Papers of George Washington, Revolutionary War Series,* Vol. 8, (Charlottesville: Univ. Press of Virginia, 1998), 428 and Robert L. Scribner and Brent Tarter, eds., "Proceedings of Fourth Virginia Convention, January 12, 1776," *Revolutionary Virginia: The Road to Independence*, Vol. 5, (University Press of Virginia, 1979), 391

Muhlenberg, who was a delegate at the 4th Convention and the minister of Beckford Parish in Dunmore County (where two of the ten companies of the 8th Virginia Regiment were raised) was selected by his fellow convention delegates in Williamsburg to command the regiment because of the esteem that many Shenandoah Valley settlers, both German and non-German, held for him. His brief service in the British army as a secretary in the 60th Regiment and his ability to speak both German and English were also important factors in Muhlenberg's selection.[7]

It is doubtful that Captain Campbell was as fluent in German as Colonel Muhlenberg, but this was not an issue because a significant number of recruits for Muhlenberg's "German Regiment" were actually of Irish, Scottish and English descent.[8] It is probable that Captain Campbell commanded a company made up of these soldiers.

Eight counties on the Virginia frontier were instructed by the Fourth Convention to select company officers (captains and lieutenants) and then raise 68 men for their allotted company.[9] Augusta County and Dunmore County were instructed to raise two companies apiece, bringing the regiment's total to ten companies of approximately 700 officers and men, provided everyone met their recruitment quotas.

---

[7] Henry A. Muhlenberg, *The Life of Major-General Peter Muhlenberg of the Revolutionary Army*, (Philadelphia, Cary and Hart, 1849), 50
[8] Brent Tarter, ed., "General Charles Lee to Edmund Pendleton, May 24, 1776," *Revolutionary Virginia: The Road to Independence,* Vol. 7, Part One, (University Press of Virginia, 1983), 248-249
[9] William W. Henings, *The Statutes at Large; Being a Collection of all the Laws of Virginia,* Vol. 9, (Richmond, 1821), 76

There is a long held and popular tradition that claims Colonel Muhlenberg recruited 300 men himself when he delivered his farewell sermon in Woodstock in late January 1776. The details of the sermon ring true; it does appear that Muhlenberg delivered an inspirational sermon to all those gathered at his church in Woodstock and that under his robe he wore a military uniform that he dramatically revealed at the sermon's conclusion. The date and impact of Muhlenberg's sermon, however, are open to some debate.

Given that the recruitment of troops was the responsibility of individual counties (specifically appointed company officers like Captain Richard Campbell chosen by county committees) and that the recruitment area of the 8th Virginia Regiment was vast, it seems unlikely that Muhlenberg's sermon (reportedly on January 23rd) convinced 300 men to join the 8th Virginia that same day.

What makes more sense is that Muhlenberg delivered his farewell sermon right before he left for Williamsburg, in March, and that about half of his regiment (300 men) had gathered in Woodstock to march east with him, which they did after he delivered his inspirational sermon. Although it seems that Captain Campbell and his company of Dunmore County men would have naturally been part of the 300 troops that marched east with Muhlenberg, it appears that they may have departed for Suffolk, the post the 8th Virginia was assigned to, ahead of Muhlenberg.[10]

---

[10] Brent Tarter, ed., "April 14, 1776" in "The Orderly Book of the Second Virginia Regiment," *The Virginia Magazine of History and Biography*, Vol. 85, (Richmond : Virginia Historical Society, 1977), 336 and Scribner and Tarter, eds., "Footnote 10," *Revolutionary Virginia: The Road to Independence*, Vol. 6, 82-83

Suffolk was situated in the southeast corner of Virginia and in the spring of 1776 was the primary post for Virginia's troops south of the James River. They were posted there to keep watch over Lord Dunmore, the British Royal Governor of Virginia. Dunmore had fled Williamsburg almost a year earlier, in June, 1775, and had attempted to establish a base of operation in Norfolk with the support of several British warships, a small detachment of British regulars, a handful of loyalist Virginians and a growing number of runaway slaves (who Dunmore offered freedom to in exchange for their service as troops). The situation looked promising for Dunmore in November 1775 as he occupied Norfolk and established control of Princess Anne and Norfolk Counties, but his stunning defeat at the Great Bridge in early December forced Dunmore and his supporters to flee to a number of vessels anchored in the Elizabeth River, just off of Norfolk and Portsmouth. A standoff ensued between Dunmore and the "rebel" troops of Virginia and North Carolina that lasted into the spring of 1776.

It was into that standoff that Captain Campbell and his company marched in mid-April 1776 when they arrived in southeastern Virginia.[11] Virginia's troops were spread throughout the south side of the James River to prevent Dunmore from staging raids onshore, so Captain Campbell's first assignment was to guard Smithfield, about twenty miles north of Suffolk.[12] Within days of their arrival, Captain Campbell and the rest of the 8th Virginia Regiment found themselves involved with a much more difficult and

---

[11] Ibid.
[12] Ibid.

unpleasant activity, the forcible evacuation of a large portion of the populations of Norfolk and Princess Ann Counties.

The ranking officer in Virginia in the spring of 1776 was Major-General Charles Lee of the Continental Army. General Lee, a former British officer with extensive military service in Europe, had served with General Washington in Massachusetts in 1775. Although he was a native of Britain and had only arrived in the colonies in 1773, Lee held the trust and admiration of many in Congress who viewed him as the most militarily experienced and knowledgeable officer in the American army.

Concern in early 1776 that the British were shifting their attention to the southern colonies prompted Congress to send General Lee southward in March to oversee the region's defenses. He arrived in Williamsburg at the end of March and soon settled his attention on Lord Dunmore. General Lee wished to deprive Dunmore of the assistance of loyalists in southern Virginia and received authorization from the Virginia Committee of Safety in mid-April to forcibly evacuate a portion of the populace of Norfolk County and Princess Anne County in order to deny Lord Dunmore much needed provisions from the local inhabitants.[13]

General Lee traveled to Suffolk on April 23rd, to personally oversee the evacuation and ordered the 8th Virginia Regiment to escort a number of wagons to Portsmouth and the surrounding area to move the, *"Beds, Cloaths, and absolute necessary cooking utensils,"* of those being forced out.[14] If

---

[13] Scribner and Tarter, eds. "Committee of Safety, April 10, 1776," *Revolutionary Virginia: Road to Independence,* Vol. 6, 369-370

[14] "General Lee to Colonel Muhlenberg, April 23, 1776," *The Lee Papers,* Vol. 1, 444

the inhabitants wished to take anything else with them, they would have to make their own arrangements.[15] The regiment was also ordered to secure all black males of military age and take them to Suffolk as a precaution.[16]

While the troops executed General Lee's orders, he received disturbing news from North Carolina. At least 3,000 British troops had reportedly landed 30 miles south of the Cape Fear River in North Carolina.[17] Leaders there urged General Lee to send help, which he did in the form of the 8th Virginia in mid-May.

General Lee accompanied the regiment on the five day march to Halifax, North Carolina, and he was not pleased by the experience. Writing to Virginia's Committee of Safety in Williamsburg a few days after they arrived in Halifax, Lee berated the 8th Virginians for their unmilitary behavior:

> *The disorderly mutinous and dangerous disposition of the soldiers of the 8th Regiment have detain'd me longer in this place than I cou'd have wish'd, more particularly as we hear (tho the accounts are not well authenticated) that the whole fleet of Transports under Lord Cornwallis is arrived at Cape Fear. We have at length after infinite trouble got this Banditti out of the Town, and of course I set out myself immediately.*[18]

---

[15] "General Lee to Colonel Muhlenberg, April 23, 1776," *The Lee Papers*, Vol. 1, 444

[16] Ibid.

[17] "Thomas Burke to General Lee, April 22, 1776," *The Lee Papers*, Vol. 1, 410-411

[18] Tarter, ed., "General Charles Lee to Edmund Pendleton, May 24, 1776," *Revolutionary Virginia: The Road to Independence*, Vol. 7, Part One, 248-249

Lee complained that desertion among the troops from the frontier was rampant and he urged Virginia's leaders to take action to halt it.

> *The spirit of desertion in these back Country troops is so alarmingly great, that I must submit it to the wisdom of the convention, whether it is not of the utmost importance to devise some means to put a stop to it, before it spreads, by enjoining the Committees of the different Counties to seize every Soldier, who cannot produce an authenticated discharge or pass....[19]*

He confessed that Virginia's civil authorities were better judges of what to do to stem the high desertion rate, but warned that

> *I can only affirm that unless some effectual method is devised and adopted, it will be impossible for us to keep the Field. The old Countrymen, particularly the Irish, whom the Officers have injudiciously inlisted in order to fill up their Companies, have much contaminated the Troops; and if more care is not taken on this head, for the future, the whole Army will be one mass of disorder, vice and confusion....[20]*

It is impossible to determine how many, if any, of Captain Campbell's troops deserted or whether any of his men had incurred General Lee's disapproval. Lee's critical reference to Irish troops, however, hints that Campbell's company may

---

[19] Tarter, ed., "General Charles Lee to Edmund Pendleton, May 24, 1776," *Revolutionary Virginia: The Road to Independence*, Vol. 7, Part One, 248-249
[20] Ibid.

have contributed to problem. Then again, the reference could also have been the result of General Lee's prejudice against the Irish.

Although General Lee held the troops of the 8th Virginia in low regard, he was careful not to include the regiment's officers in his criticism, writing that,

> *Altho I have so great reason to complain of the misconduct of this Regiment, I must do the Officers (particularly the Field Officers) the justice to say, that their conduct is in general very satisfactory.*[21]

About a week after General Lee's letter to the Committee of Safety, he ordered the 8th Virginia to march even further south, to Charleston, South Carolina. Lee correctly deduced that Charleston was the true objective of the British force in the Carolinas and he rushed ahead to get there in time to prevent its capture.[22] Captain Campbell and his fellow 8th Virginians grudgingly trailed behind Lee and reached Charleston two weeks after Lee's arrival on June 8th.

The 8th Virginia in Charleston

When the 8th Virginia arrived in Charleston on June 23, the British under General Henry Clinton and General Charles Lord Cornwallis, were well on their way to launching an attack on the outer defenses of the city. The key patriot defensive position protecting Charleston was a fort made of

---

[21] Ibid.
[22] "General Lee to Edmund Pendleton, June 1, 1776," *The Lee Papers*, Vol. 2, 51

palmetto log walls (filled with sand) that were sixteen feet thick and capable of absorbing the heavy cannon blasts of the British navy.[23] A garrison of only 350 South Carolina troops manned the 31 cannon in the fort, but they were supported by a large detachment of 750 troops on the north end of the island who were positioned to prevent a British landing from an adjacent island.[24]

Such a landing was exactly what the British intended to do with their 2,200 troops.[25] The plan called for the British navy to pound the rebel fort with cannon fire while the British army crossed a narrow cut of water that separated Sullivan Island from Long Island (upon which the British army had landed weeks earlier) then march four miles to the fort and capture it by storm.

Colonel Muhlenberg's Virginians were not initially deployed on Sullivan Island, but rather, at Haddrell's Point on the mainland to guard against a possible British crossing from the outer islands.[26] When the British navy commenced its attack upon the American fort on Sullivan Island on June 28th, Captain Campbell and his fellow 8th Virginians were spectators.

The British attack unraveled quickly, however, when General Clinton discovered that he had no way to cross the cut between Sullivan's and Long Island without suffering unacceptably high losses. The narrow channel between the two islands was deeper than Clinton had been informed (seven

---

[23] Edwin C. Bearss, *The Battle of Sullivan's Island and the Capture of Fort Moultrie: A Documented Narrative and Troop Movement Maps*, (U.S. Dept. of the Interior, 1968), 58-59
[24] Ibid., 57, 59-60
[25] Ibid., 29, 50
[26] Ibid., 61

feet at low tide) and thus unfordable, and the British commander believed any attempt to use boats to either cross the cut or land further up the island would lead to enormous casualties among his troops.[27] So with Commodore Peter Parker's warships fully engaged against the fort, the best General Clinton could do was create a distraction by threatening to cross the cut, thereby keeping the 750 rebel infantry at the cut away from their fort.

The outcome of the battle thus depended on the British warships under Commodore Parker and Colonel William Moultrie's garrison inside the fort. Relatively safe behind their sixteen foot thick walls (that simply absorbed many of the British cannon balls) the American garrison punished the stationary British warships with 26 pound, 18 pound, 12 pound, and 9 pound ordinance.[28] Several of Commodore Parker's frigates attempted to sail past the fort but became grounded in low water and fell out of action. One of these was eventually abandoned and burned.

General Lee, who was on the mainland when the attack began, crossed over to Sullivan's Island around 5 p.m. and was pleased to see that Colonel Moultrie had the situation well in hand.[29] Moultrie had lost over a score of men, but he was confident that the damage his men inflicted upon the enemy was far worse.[30] On that count Moultrie was correct for the

---

[27] William J. Morgan, ed., "Comments by Major General Henry Clinton Upon the Naval Attack on Sullivan's Island, June 28, 1776," and "Major General Henry Clinton to Lord George Germain, July 8, 1776," *Naval Documents of the American Revolution,* Vol. 5, (Washington: 1970), 802 and 983

[28] Bearss, 58-59

[29] Ibid., 84-85

[30] "General Lee to the President of the Virginia Convention, June 29," 1776," *The Lee Papers,* Vol. 2, 93

American fire did significantly more damage to the British navy than Commodore Parker's fire did to the fort.

General Lee was surprised and impressed at the resolve of the garrison and described the engagement as, *"one of the most furious cannonades I ever heard or saw."*[31] Lee admitted after the battle that,

> *The behavior of the Garrison, both men and officers, with Colonel Moultrie at their head, I confess astonished me; it was brave to the last degree. I had no idea so much coolness and intrepidity could be displayed by a collection of raw recruits, as I was witness of in this garrison.*[32]

Up to this point of the battle, the 8th Virginians had remained on the mainland, in reserve. Late in the afternoon, General Lee ordered Colonel Muhlenberg to reinforce the large American detachment defending the cut at the northern end of Sullivan Island.[33] Muhlenberg's men must have displayed some zeal to join the fight for General Lee paid them a compliment in his report to the Virginia Convention after the battle:

> *I know not which Corps I have the greatest reason to be pleased with, Muhlenberg's Virginians, or the North Carolina troops. – they are both equally alert, zealous and spirited.*[34]

---

[31] "General Lee to the President of the Virginia Convention, June 29, 1776," *The Lee Papers,* Vol. 2, 93
[32] Ibid.
[33] Bearss, 86
[34] "General Lee to the President of the Virginia Convention, June 29, 1776," *The Lee Papers,* Vol. 2, 93

Muhlenberg's Virginians may have been spirited and eager to join the fight, but it appears they saw little actual action on Sullivan's Island. The honors of the day belonged to Colonel Moultrie's garrison, who withstood the British navy's intense bombardment and returned fire with such deadly effect that Commodore Parker eventually disengaged and withdrew. The British threat to Charleston thus ended in defeat for the attackers, who suffered significant damage to their ships and heavy losses among their crews.

The damage to the British navy was so great that they did not make another attempt at Charlestown. After three weeks of repairs to their ships, the British sailed away from Charleston and the South.[35] It was time to join General William Howe in New York.[36]

The departure of the British caused General Lee to turn his attention to neighboring Georgia. Officials there had expressed concerns about their defenseless state and appealed for assistance against the British navy, Indians allied with the British, and from British troops operating from St. Augustine and several smaller outposts in East Florida.[37]

By the end of July, General Lee had resolved to march to Georgia with a force that included the 8th Virginians. Colonel Muhlenberg's regiment was much reduced by the rigors of service in the field with over 150 men unfit for duty due to illness.[38] Major Peter Helpenstine became so ill he resigned

---

[35] Bearss, 102-105
[36] Ibid., 106
[37] "General Lee to President Rutledge, July 22, 1776," *The Lee Papers*, Vol. 2, 159
[38] Charles H. Lesser, ed., "Monthly Return of the Forces in South Carolina, July 1776," *The Sinews of Independence: Monthly Strength Reports of the Continental Army*, (University of Chicago Press, 1976), 27

his commission in early August and returned to Virginia, but died soon after.[39]

General Lee appointed Richard Campbell acting Major of the 8th Virginia on August 10th, (pending the approval of Congress). Although Congress would confirm Campbell's appointment, several captains of the 8th Virginia who outranked Campbell took umbrage with his promotion and the matter was ultimately settled, mostly in Campbell's favor, by General Washington in late 1777.[40]

General Lee was eager to strike the British in East Florida to put a stop to their harassment of Georgia. This largely wilderness region between Georgia and the British stronghold at St. Augustine held several British outposts from which incursions into Georgia had been launched. The losses suffered by Georgians from these British raids involved mostly slaves and cattle, but the potential for greater loss was high, so General Lee resolved to break up the British posts in East Florida.[41]

Supply and transport delays pushed General Lee's march to Georgia into mid-August.[42] The 8th Virginia, with approximately 300 men fit for duty, made up part of Lee's force and soon after they reached Savannah, Lee ordered the

---

[39] Francis, B. Heitman, *Historical Register of Officers of the Continental Army During the War of the Revolution, April 1775 to December 1783*, Washington, D.C., 1914, 284

[40] Ford, ed., "Resolution of Congress, January 21, 1777," *Journals of the Continental Congress,* Vol. 7, 52 and Philander D. Chase,., ed. "John Hancock to General Washington, May 15, 1777," *The Papers of George Washington,* Vol. 9 (Charlottesville: Univ. Press of Virginia, 1999), 430

[41] "General Lee to Richard Peters, August 2, 1776," *The Lee Papers,* Vol. 2, 188-189

[42] "Orders Issued on the Expedition to Georgia, August 12 and 16, 1776," *The Lee Papers*, Vol. 2, 251-252

Virginians further south another 30 miles to the settlement of Sunbury.[43] Little of note occurred on the march, and the 8th Virginia was recalled to Savannah where they learned that Congress had ordered General Lee to return to Philadelphia, effectively ending his expedition to Georgia.[44]

A few weeks earlier, General Lee had issued orders to send Colonel Muhlenberg's sick and unfit Virginians who had remained in Charleston (approximately 150 men) back to Virginia as soon as they recovered.[45] Colonel Muhlenberg and an unknown number of his men also marched north upon General Lee's departure, leaving Major Campbell and the remainder of the 8th Virginia behind in Charleston.[46] Upon his return to Virginia in December, Colonel Muhlenberg wrote to his father and described the, *"arduous campaign"* that he and his troops had endured in the South.[47]

In late January, Congress ordered Major Campbell and the remainder of the 8th Virginia in South Carolina to also return to Virginia. In the same dispatch, Congress approved Richard Campbell's appointment as Major.

---

[43] Lesser, ed., "Monthly Return of the Forces in South Carolina, July 1776," *The Sinews of Independence: Monthly Strength Reports of the Continental Army*, 27 and "Orders Issued on the Expedition to Georgia, August 21, 1776," *The Lee Papers*, Vol. 2, 253

[44] Ford., ed., John Hancock to General Lee, August 8, 1776," *Journals of the Continental Congress*, Vol. 5, 639 and "Orders, September 9, 1776," *The Lee Papers*, Vol. 2, 258-259

[45] "General Lee to General Armstrong, August 15, 1776, *The Lee Papers*, Vol. 2, 230

[46] Muhlenberg, "Colonel Muhlenberg to his Father, December 20, 1776," *The Life of Major-General Peter Muhlenberg of the Revolutionary Army*, 69 and Ford, ed., "Resolution of Congress, January 21, 1777," *Journals of the Continental Congress*, Vol. 7, 52

[47] Muhlenberg, "Peter Muhlenberg to Henry Muhlenberg, December 20, 1776," *The Life of Major-General Peter Muhlenberg of the Revolutionary Army*, 69

> *That Major Richard Campbell, who was appointed by General Lee in South Carolina, to act as major to Colonel Muhlenburgh's regiment, until the pleasure of Congress should be known, be appointed to said majority, his commission to bear* [the] *date to 10 of August last, the time he was appointed in general orders.*[48]

Congress also authorized an advance of $300 to Major Campbell,

> *To enable him to discharge waggons, and furnish the troops he has now with him on the way to camp, with shoes, and other necessaries as they may want; the said Major Campbell to be accountable for the expenditure.*[49]

A month passed before Major Campbell and his command reached home. Colonel Muhlenberg reported their arrival to General Washington in late February.

> *The detachment from the southward arrived here this week in a shattered condition, having only seventy men fit for duty; so that it will be almost impossible to march the men so soon as I could wish.*[50]

---

[48] Ford, ed., "Resolution of Congress, January 21, 1777," *Journals of the Continental Congress,* Vol. 7, 52

[49] Ibid.

[50] Frank E. Grizzard, ed., "Colonel Muhlenberg to General Washington, February 23, 1777," *The Papers of George Washington, Revolutionary War Series,* Vol. 8, (Charlottesville: University Press of Virginia, 1998), 428

Muhlenberg added that he had three full companies ready to march to New Jersey. He also offered an observation and request that he thought would improve his regiment.

> *The whole Regt at present consists of Riflemen, & The Campaign we made to the Southward last Summer fully convinces me, that on a march where Soldiers are without Tents, & their Arms continually exposd to the Weather; Rifles are of little use, I would therefore request Your Excellency to Convert my Regt into Musketry.*[51]

Although there is no record of General Washington ordering a change of arms for the entire 8th Virginia, it is likely that a large number of Muhlenberg's troops were issued muskets in place of their rifles. At least one company of the regiment, however, Captain James Knox's company from Fincastle, retained their rifles to serve in Colonel Daniel Morgan's select rifle corps that was formed in the summer of 1777.[52] In the woods of New York and the battlefields of Saratoga, they would prove the utility of their rifles in battle.

---

[51] Grizzard, ed., "Colonel Muhlenberg to General Washington, February 23, 1777," *The Papers of George Washington, Revolutionary War Series,* Vol. 8, 428

[52] Michael Cecere, *They Are Indeed a Very Useful Corps: American Riflemen in the Revolutionary War,* (Heritage Books, 2006), 203

Virginia in 1776

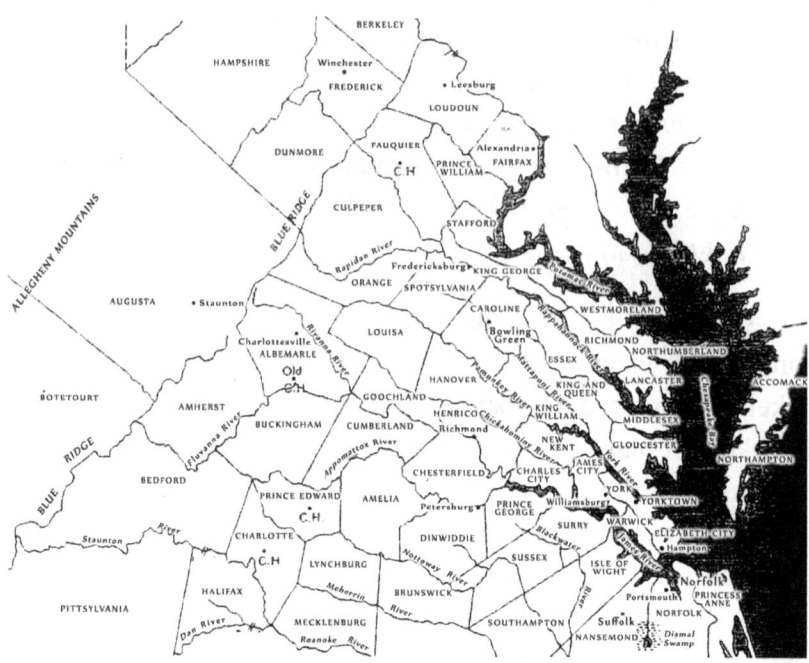

Chapter Two

I am intent on giving the Enemy Battle Wherever I should meet them.

1777

Major Richard Campbell spent approximately two months in Virginia recovering from his long deployment in South Carolina. While he rested and recruited for the regiment, his promotion in the 8th Virginia was challenged by several Virginia officers who believed they outranked Campbell and deserved promotion ahead of him. Even Campbell's commander, Colonel Peter Muhlenberg, apparently expressed concern about Campbell's promotion.

A letter to Muhlenberg written by George Johnston, one of General Washington's aide-de-camps, hinted that Muhlenberg had expressed his concern and perhaps even his objection to General Washington of Richard Campbell's promotion. Johnston informed Muhlenberg that General Washington could do nothing about Campbell's promotion because Congress had already approved it.

> *Congress having confirmed Majr. Campbell in his Office, leaves his Excellency no power to remove him, but for the Commission of some Offense.*[1]

Numerous vacancies throughout the American army caused by death, illness, resignation, and promotion prompted a significant reorganization of Washington's officer corps in the

---

[1] Frank E. Grizzard, ed., "George Johnston to Colonel Muhlenberg, March 9, 1777," *The Papers of George Washington*, Vol. 8, 419

spring of 1777 which seemed to settle the controversy over Major Campbell's promotion in his favor. Colonel Muhlenberg was promoted to brigadier-general, which meant that command of the 8th Virginia went to Lieutenant Colonel Abraham Bowman, who was himself promoted to Colonel.[2] Major John Markham of the 2nd Virginia Regiment was promoted to Lieutenant Colonel and transferred to the 8th Virginia while Major Campbell retained his position in the 8th Virginia, much to the continued displeasure of several Virginia officers who insisted they were senior to him.[3]

At the urging of at least some of these disgruntled officers, Congress re-visited the matter in May, requesting that General Washington inquire into the dispute over Major Campbell's commission and if Washington found that Campbell's promotion, *"was out of course,"* it would be, *"rendered null and void.*[4]

After several months, General Washington apparently found that Campbell's promotion was indeed, *"out of course,"* but he did not act upon the matter until late September, when, in his general orders for September 29, 1777 he referred to, *"Capt: Campbell of the 8th,"* and announced that Campbell had been promoted to, *"the Major of the 13th V—regiment."*[5]

In the months prior to his promotion, General Washington had referred to Campbell several times as Major and Campbell

---

[2] Grizzard, ed., "General Orders, March 22, 1777," *The Papers of George Washington,* Vol. 8, 614

[3] Ibid.

[4] Philander P. Chase, ed., "John Hancock to General Washington, May 15, 1777," *The Papers of George Washington,* Vol. 9, (Charlottesville: University Press of Virginia, 1999), 430 and "Footnote 1," 439

[5] Philander D. Chase and Edward G. Lengel, eds., "General Orders, September 29, 1777," *The Papers of George* Washington, Vol. 11, (Charlottesville: University Press of Virginia, 2001), 343

served as such in the 8th Virginia through the battle of Brandywine in September. Washington's reference to Captain Campbell in his general orders of September 29th, may have stung Campbell, but it was meant as a nod to the other Virginia officers who had maintained all along that Campbell's field promotion to Major of the 8th Virginia in the summer of 1776 was invalid. Campbell's new commission as major and his transfer to the 13th Virginia Regiment finally put the matter to rest.

Prior to this happy resolution for Major Campbell, he struggled with the rest of the American army to stop the British from marching on Philadelphia.

The Philadelphia Campaign of 1777

General Washington's army in New Jersey grew steadily in strength over the spring of 1777. By early May, the men of the 8th Virginia numbered 134 in camp, but Major Campbell was apparently not one of them.[6] By the end of the month, however, Campbell had joined the regiment, which had grown to nearly 200 men, a far cry from its authorized full strength of 700 but about average for the Virginia regiments that had been

---

[6] Lesser, ed., "A Return of the Troops…Under Command of Major-General Lincoln, May 3, 1777," *The Sinews of Independence: Monthly Strength Reports of the Continental Army*, 45, and Chase, ed., "General Washington to Colonels Alexander Spotswood, Alexander McClanachan, and Abraham Bowman and Lieutenant Colonel Christian Febiger, April 30, 1777," *The Papers of George Washington*, Vol. 9, 315

Note: In his letter to the above colonels, General Washington asked each to select four trusted men to serve on his life guard. As the 8th Virginia only had one staff officer on its May 3, 1777 return, it is safe to conclude that Colonel Bowman was that officer and Major Campbell had not reached camp yet.

on campaign for a year as the 8th Virginia had been in South Carolina.[7]

The steady growth of his army allowed General Washington to reorganize his force. Major Campbell's 8th Virginia was brigaded with the 4th Virginia, the 12th Virginia, and a combined regiment of Delaware, Pennsylvanian, and New Jersey troops under Colonel John Patten.[8] An additional Virginia Regiment under Colonel William Grayson was also brigaded with the 8th Virginia, but had yet to arrive in camp.[9]

The brigade commander was General Charles Scott, who, by mid-1777 had two years of valuable command experience under him. Scott led a company of independent militia from Cumberland County to Williamsburg in the summer of 1775 before any Virginia regiments of regulars were even formed. When the 1st and 2nd Virginia Regiments were formed in the fall of 1775, Scott was appointed to the 2nd Virginia Regiment as its Lieutenant Colonel. In 1776, Scott was promoted to colonel and assumed command of the 5th Virginia Regiment. Finally, in the winter of 1777, Scott was promoted to brigadier-general by Congress and assigned to Virginia's 4th brigade.

General Scott and his fellow officers kept very busy in May and early June, organizing their units and preparing for the upcoming campaign. Major Campbell and the 8th Virginia

---

[7] Lesser, ed., "A General Return of the Continental Forces, May 21, 1777," *The Sinews of Independence: Monthly Strength Reports of the Continental Army*, 48
Note: All three regimental staff officers were in camp according to the Troop Return for May 21, 1777
[8] Chase, ed., "Arrangement and Present Strength of the Army in New Jersey, May 20, 1777," *The Papers of George Washington*, Vol. 9, 492
[9] Ibid.

apparently had gone without tents for more than a month and did not receive an allotment of them (36) until May.[10] At six men to a tent, that was likely sufficient to shelter the entire regiment then in camp.

While Washington's army grew stronger in camp among the Watchtung Mountains of New Jersey, General William Howe and the thousands of British and Hessian troops under his command occupied New Brunswick, New Jersey just a few miles away. Howe sought to draw Washington out from his strong defensive position in the mountains and marched his army towards the Delaware River and Philadelphia on June 13th.

Washington refused to commit his army to a general engagement against General Howe's stronger force and sent only light parties forward to skirmish with the British. It appears that Major Campbell was involved with the skirmishing, for on June 16th, Campbell informed General Washington in a dispatch that the enemy was marching towards the position of Colonel Daniel Morgan's Rife Corps at Van Vecter's Bridge.[11] A week of skirmishing ensued with little advantage to either side. Frustrated, General Howe disengaged and withdrew back to New Brunswick. Then, inexplicably, he abandoned New Brunswick and marched to Perth Amboy which was situated opposite of Staten Island.

Howe's withdrawal, which reduced the threat to Washington's army, allowed General Scott to order Major Campbell back to Virginia to, *"Superintend, & Inspect into the*

---

[10] Chase, ed., "General Mifflin to General Washington, May 27, 1777," *The Papers of George Washington*, Vol. 9, 543

[11] Frank E. Grizzard, ed., "General Washington to General Lincoln and General Wayne, June 16, 1777," *The Papers of George Washington*, Vol. 10, (Charlottesville: University Press of Virginia, 2000), 52

Conduct & proceedings of the Officers of the 8th Regimt & to Transmit an account of their Conduct & success in recruiting to Head Quarters, once a Month...."[12]

One month into this assignment, Campbell wrote to General Washington from Woodstock, Virginia with an update and a request.

> *I have examined into their Success, & find that the Recruiting Service goes on very slowly. There is a great number of Officers of our Regimt from Camp in this State, & no probability of raising Men by that Means – Capt. Higgins & the Officers of his Company...have not raised more than 20 Men in the course of five months. Tho' the greatest Industry had been used by them. The other Officers ordered from Camp have met with less success. Our Assembly have fallen on ways to fill up our Battalions, which I hope will render it unnecessary to keep so many Officers on the Recruiting Service, as are now absent from the 8th Regiment.*
>
> *Things thus circumstanced make me wish to return to my post, will thank your Excellency for orders to do so, the draughts will take place the 10th of next Month, which I hope will answer the purpose intended. Till I receive your Orders, shall continue to use my endeavours to forward the recruiting Business, tho' have no prospect of being successful.*[13]

---

[12] Grizzard, ed., "Major Campbell to General Washington,, July 24, 1777," *The Papers of George Washington*, Vol. 10, 382
[13] Ibid.

General Washington replied to Major Campbell through an aide who wrote on August 4th that,

> *Your Letter of 24th July was handed to his Excelly yesterday, in Answer to which I am direct'd to Inform you that you are immediately to return to Camp with the other Officers of your Corps & Join your Regiment.*[14]

Re-joining the American army likely proved more difficult than expected for Major Campbell, for Washington's army spent much of the summer of 1777 on the march. When Washington's aide, Lieutenant Colonel Fitzgerald penned General Washington's orders to Major Campbell, the American army was camped outside Philadelphia, resting from a forced march across New Jersey. General Washington was baffled at the conduct of his adversary, General Howe. In early July the bulk of the British army had boarded British ships and disappeared over the horizon, and General Washington had spent the next six weeks trying to determine their destination.

It is difficult to say when Major Campbell re-joined the American army. As it appears it took his letter ten days to reach Washington, Campbell likely received his orders to return to the army in mid-August. He probably took a day or two to arrange his affairs at home, and then another week to ten days to track down the army, which, by late August was in Delaware, reacting to the British landing at Head of Elk, Maryland.

---

[14] Grizzard, ed., "Lieutenant Colonel John Fitzgerald to Major Campbell, August 4, 1777," *The Papers of George Washington*, Vol. 10, 383

Although we cannot precisely determine when Campbell rejoined the army, it is very probable that he was back with the 8th Virginia Regiment in time to participate in one of the largest battles of the Revolutionary War, the Battle of Brandywine.

Battle of Brandywine

When General Howe and approximately 15,000 British and German troops landed at Head of Elk, Maryland in late August 1777, it was clear that Philadelphia was their target. General Washington rushed his army into Delaware in response and an engagement erupted between advance units of the two sides at Cooches Bridge. General Howe's troops pushed the Americans back, but then, after a week of relative inactivity, instead of moving forward in a northeasterly direction to attack Washington's main army, General Howe marched due north to get around Washington's right flank.

The American commander realized the danger and moved north, determined to keep his army between the British and Philadelphia.[15] He halted at Chads's Ford on Brandywine Creek, just over the border of Delaware into Pennsylvania, and deployed his army along the east side of the creek to defend the road to Philadelphia.

General Anthony Wayne's brigade of Pennsylvanians defended Chads's Ford itself while General Nathanael Greene's division of Virginians (comprised of General George Weedon's and General Peter Muhlenberg's brigades) defended the ground to Wayne's left, immediately south of the

---

[15] Chase and Lengel, eds., "General Washington to General Smallwood, September 9, 1777," *The Papers of George Washington,* Vol. 11, 179-180

ford. General John Sullivan's division of Maryland troops was posted a mile north of Chads's Ford to guard another ford there as well as Washington's right flank.[16]

General Adam Stephen's division of General Scott's and General Woodford's brigades, as well as General William Alexander (Lord Stirling's) division of Pennsylvania and New Jersey troops, were posted in reserve on a hill overlooking Brandywine Creek, just north of Chads's Ford. The evening of September 10th, 1777 was undoubtedly an anxious one for Major Campbell and the men of the 8th Virginia Regiment as they waited with the rest of General Scott's brigade on the hills overlooking Brandywine Creek.

With battle imminent, General Washington had posted General William Maxwell's 1,000 man light corps across Brandywine Creek to watch the enemy's movements and harass them if and when they moved against the Americans. Maxwell's men did not have long to wait; General Howe ordered a column of his army forward at daybreak on September 11th. Shortly after dawn gunfire erupted in the countryside well west of Brandywine Creek.

While Maxwell's light corps engaged the advance troops of General Howe's army, the bulk of the British forces, led by General Howe himself, marched along a circuitous route to gain Washington's right flank and replicate Howe's rout of Washington at Long Island in 1776. General Washington actually anticipated Howe's movement and hoped to turn it against him by striking at Howe's weakened force to Washington's front, but faulty intelligence on whether Howe had actually divided his army paralyzed Washington with

---

[16] Thomas McGuire, *The Philadelphia Campaign: Brandywine and the Fall of Philadelphia*, Vol. 1, (Stackpole Books, 2006), 170-171, 197

indecision. As a result, the opportunity slipped away and by the afternoon Washington was scrambling to reposition his troops to protect his threatened right flank.

With more than half of the British army bearing down on his right and rear, General Washington ordered General Stephen and General Stirling to march their divisions northeastwards to the heights near Birmingham Meeting House in order to head off the British. General Sullivan was ordered to follow with his division and assume overall command of the redeployed right wing of Washington's army.

These troops rushed to the village of Dilworth, three miles in their rear, then swung north towards a hill overlooking Birmingham Meeting House and a road running north to Osborne Hill, where General Howe and 8,000 British and German troops had paused to rest after their long march around the American army.

General Stephen initially posted his men upon a large, cleared, hill just west of the Birmingham Road. He held the right of the American line. General Woodford's brigade was posted on the right flank of the American line; General Scott's brigade (with Major Campbell and the 8th Virginians) formed on Woodford's left and General Stirling's division formed to Scott's left. General Sullivan's division scrambled into position to the left of Stirling just as General Howe's troops advanced against them. Sullivan's arrival forced the entire American line to shift right a few hundred yards and actually placed General Scott's and General Woodford's brigades in a stronger defensive position.

A British light infantry officer who participated in the assault on the right side of the American line recalled that, *"The position the enemy had taken was very strong indeed --*

very commanding ground, a wood on their rear and flanks, a ravine and strong paling [fence] *in front.*"[17] Captain John Montresor, General Howe's chief engineer, also noted the difficult terrain on the American right and acknowledged its impact on the engagement.

> *The ground on the left* [which would have been the American right] *being the most difficult, the rebels disputed it with the Light Infantry with great spirit, particularly their officers....*[18]

Major Campbell and his fellow officers in the 8th Virginia were likely some of the spirited American officers defending the right side of the American line at Birmingham Heights with General Scott's brigade.

Unfortunately for the Americans, General Sullivan's division on the other side of the line never fully deployed before the British attacked and many of his men fell into disorder. General Sullivan, who had taken position near a battery of five cannon in the center of the entire American line to superintend the overall fight, sent his aides to reform his division, but they had little success and most of Sullivan's troops withdrew in disarray.

With British troops attacking on their front and now upon their exposed left flank, the pressure on General Stirling's men in the center of the American line overwhelmed them and they also gave way. To Stirling's right, however, remained Stephen's division with General Scott and Woodford at the head of their brigades.

---

[17] McGuire, 216
[18] Ibid.

The fight on the American right was severe, made more so upon the British by American cannon that played very effectively upon the British. A British officer who experienced the cannon fire recalled that,

> *There was a most infernal Fire of Cannon & musketry – smoak – incessant shouting – incline to the right! Incline to the Left! – halt! – charge!...The trees* [were] *cracking over ones head. The branches riven by the artillery, the leaves falling as in autumn by the grapeshot.*[19]

General Stephen's Virginians were well served by the artillery which, along with heavy musket and rifle fire, initially kept the British and German troops to their front at bay. A German officer noted that, *"The small arms fire was terrible, the counter-fire from the enemy, especially against us, was the most concentrated."* [20]

The collapse of the American left flank and center, however, left Stephen's Virginians in an impossible situation. A British officer described the final assault on their position.

> *They stood the charge till we came to the last* [fence]. *Their line then began to break, and a general retreat took place soon after, except for their guns, many of which were defended to the last, indeed several officers were cut down at the guns.*[21]

---

[19] McGuire, 216
[20] Ibid., 237
[21] Ibid., 238

Although American reinforcements under General Greene arrived in time to screen the American withdrawal, the fighting for Major Campbell and the 8th Virginians was over for the day. General Washington withdrew his army towards Philadelphia to regroup.

Anticipating that General Howe would attempt to cross the Schuylkill River above Philadelphia, General Washington marched his battered army eastward to Chester. The next day he crossed the Schuylkill River via a pontoon bridge and marched northwest past Philadelphia to the falls of the river near Germanton.

Washington and his army then re-crossed the Schuylkill River on September 14th, and marched southwestward, *"intent on giving the Enemy Battle wherever I should meet them."*[22] General Howe and his troops remained in the vicinity of Dilworth for several days following the battle, but just as General Washington expected, when Howe did finally march, it was in a northeasterly direction towards the upper fords of the Schuylkill River.

The two armies nearly clashed a few miles southwest of Valley Forge, but, *"a most violent Flood of Rain,"* damaged the bulk of the American army's musket cartridges and caused Washington to disengage and withdraw northward to Yellow Springs.[23] Concerned that General Howe was maneuvering to flank him (as he had at Brandywine and Brooklyn) Washington marched further northwestward.[24]

---

[22] Chase and Lengel, eds., "General Washington to John Hancock, September 23, 1777," *The Papers of George Washington, Revolutionary Series*, Vol. 11, 301

[23] Ibid.

[24] Chase and Lengel, eds., "General Washington to John Hancock, September 18, 1777," *The Papers of George Washington*, Vol. 11, 262

Philadelphia Falls

General Washington was unsure of General Howe's true objective; the British commander had placed his army about mid-way between the American capital at Philadelphia and a vital American supply depot at Reading. Having been burned twice by General Howe's flanking movements, Washington was determined not to be outflanked again. When British troop movements on September 21st, suggested that Reading was Howe's true objective, Washington acted quickly and shifted his army closer to Reading.[25]

Unfortunately for the Americans, General Washington had miscalculated. General Howe was not interested in the supplies at Reading; Philadelphia was his true objective, and his army reversed direction and crossed the Schuylkill River south of Washington unopposed.[26] General Washington sheepishly informed Congress, which had removed to Lancaster days earlier, of this development.

> *The Enemy, by a variety of perplexing Maneuvres thro' a County from which I could not derive the least intelligence being to a man disaffected, contrived to pass the Schuylkill last Night at the Flat land and other Fords in the Neighbourhood of it. They marched immediately towards Philada and I imagine their advanced parties will be near that City to Night. They had so far got the Start before I recd certain intelligence...that I found it in vain to think of overtaking their Rear with Troops*

---

[25] McGuire., 320
[26] Ibid., 322

> *harassed as ours had been with constant marching since the Battle of Brandywine....*[27]

General Washington felt obligated to offer an explanation of how he found himself out of position to challenge the British crossing of the Schuylkill.

> *The day before yesterday they were again in motion and marched rapidly up the Road leading towards Reading. This induced me to believe that they had two objects in view, one to get round the right of the Army, the other perhaps to detach parties to Reading where we had considerable quantities of military Stores. To frustrate those intentions I moved the Army up on this side of the River to this place* [Pottsgrove] *determined to keep pace with them, but early this morning I recd intelligence that they had crossed at the Fords below.*[28]

Addressing a question Washington was sure the entire Congress was thinking, he added,

> *Why I did not follow immediately I have mentioned in the former part of my letter. But the strongest Reason against being able to make a forced march is the want of Shoes;...at least one thousand Men are bare footed and have performed the marches in that condition.*[29]

---

[27] Chase and Lengel, eds., "General Washington to John Hancock, September 23, 1777," *The Papers of George Washington, Revolutionary Series*, Vol. 11, 301-302
[28] Ibid.
[29] Ibid.

All General Washington could do was move closer to the British in Philadelphia and await either reinforcements or a more favorable opportunity to strike.[30] While he waited, Washington reshuffled some of his officers, including Richard Campbell, who was officially promoted to the rank of Major and transferred to the 13th Virginia Regiment.[31]

---

[30] Chase and Lengel, eds., "Council of War," September 28, 1777," *The Papers of George Washington, Revolutionary Series*, Vol. 11, 338-339

[31] Chase and Lengel, eds., "General Orders, September 29, 1777," *The Papers of George Washington, Revolutionary Series,* Vol. 11, 343

Pennsylvania

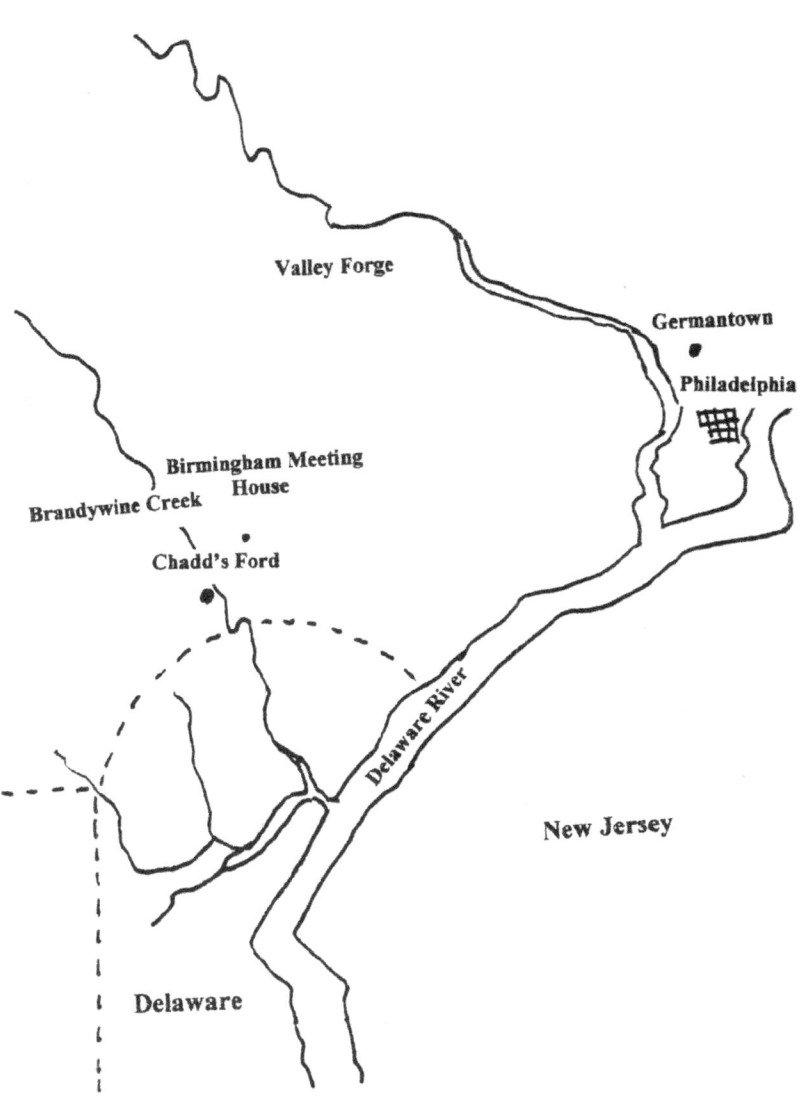

Chapter Three

[Major] *Campbell Behaved Gallantly During the Action*

1777-1778

The 13th Virginia Regiment was perhaps the most frontier oriented regiment in the continental army with soldiers recruited from the West Augusta District of Virginia (basically portions of present day Ohio, western Pennsylvania and West Virginia). The Virginia legislature had only recently created three new counties out of the district, Yohogania, Monogalia, and Ohio counties, and it was from here that the men of the 13th Virginia Regiment were raised.[1]

Colonel William Russell commanded the regiment, his second in command was Lieutenant Colonel George Gibson. The 13th Virginia was formed in the spring of 1777 as one of six additional regiments authorized by Virginia's government at the end of 1776. They mustered at Fort Pitt in early 1777 and like all of the new Virginia regiments, joined General Washington's army in New Jersey in piecemeal detachments during the spring and summer.

Interestingly, several companies of the regiment never left Fort Pitt, not because they were posted there, but because their officers failed to raise an adequate number of troops (or desertion drew off those who did join). More than a year after

---

[1] Robert K. Wright, Jr., *The Continental Army*, (Washington, D.C.: Center of Military History, U.S. Army, 1983), 291

the regiment was formed, General Washington noted that there was still, "*upwards of 100 of the 13 Virginia now at & near Fort Pitt, & many deserters...*"[2]

When Major Campbell joined the regiment in late September, the 13th Virginia was well under half its authorized strength.[3] They were part of General Peter Muhlenberg's brigade. Muhlenberg was Major Campbell's original commander in the 8th Virginia Regiment as well as his former minister in Woodstock, Virginia. Within a week of their "reunion" they were on the march with the rest of General Washington's army to strike the enemy outside of Philadelphia and, hopefully, avenge Washington's loss of Philadelphia and defeat at Brandywine.

Battle of Germantown

Two developments occurred in late September that convinced General Washington to launch a surprise attack upon the British outside Philadelphia. A brigade of Connecticut continentals (about 1,000 strong) that had been posted in the New York Highlands arrived in camp at about the same time General Howe sent 1,000 British soldiers from Philadelphia to Chester, Pennsylvania to deal with several

---

[2] Edward G. Lengel, ed., "General Washington to Timothy Pickering, May 23, 1778," *The Papers of George Washington,* Vol. 15, (Charlottesville: University Press of Virginia, 2006), 204-205

[3] Lesser, ed., "A General Return of the Continental Army...Dec. 1, 1777," *The Sinews of Independence,* 54

Note: Although the author does not have a troop return for October or November, returns for December 1777, March 1778 and May 1778 remain relatively consistent that the troop strength of the 13th Regiment with General Washington's army was less than 200 men.

American river forts that prevented the British navy from sailing up the Delaware River to Philadelphia.[4]

The 2,000 man troop swing in General Washington's favor persuaded him to strike at the British. His plan called for the army to march throughout the night in several separate columns and converge on the bulk of the British army, which was encamped several miles north of Philadelphia in the village of Germantown, at dawn. It was to be a reprise of Trenton, without the difficult river crossing or storm.

General Sullivan commanded the right wing of Washington's army. His force comprised his own division of Maryland troops along with General Wayne's Pennsylvania division. General Greene commanded the left wing of Washington's army which included his division (of Muhlenberg's and Weedon's brigades) and General Stephen's two Virginia brigades). The recently arrived brigade of Connecticut continentals under General Alexander McDougall also marched with Greene's force, but they were to file off and attack the enemy's right flank (with the militia) as soon as the fighting began.[5]

General Greene's wing had the longest route to march to get into position, so they started at 6 p.m. As there was no moon that evening, the men struggled in the dark over bad roads.[6]

---

[4] Thomas J. McGuire, *The Philadelphia Campaign: Germantown and the Roads to Valley Forge*, Vol. 2, (Stackpole Books, 2007), 45-46

[5] Chase and Lengel, eds., "General Orders for Attacking Germantown, Oct. 3, 1777," *The Papers of George Washington, Revolutionary Series*, Vol. 11, 375

[6] McGuire, *The Philadelphia Campaign: Germantown and the Roads to Valley Forge*, Vol. 2, 52-53

By 5 a.m. the next morning, three of Washington's four columns were in position to attack. General Greene's column, however, had fallen behind and was late. That didn't stop General Sullivan with the right wing of Washington's army from proceeding as planned. He approached General Howe's light infantry outposts, which were situated about two miles north of the British main camp in Germantown, just after 5 a.m. A thick fog coupled with the dim light of dawn obscured visibility, but General Sullivan had superior numbers and he pressed on in the face of scattered enemy musket fire from the British picket line and cannon fire from two 6 pound cannon.[7]

The British 2nd light battalion was now alarmed, but they were also significantly outnumbered and had no chance of stopping Sullivan's men. The British gave ground and retreated to Benjamin Chew's large stone mansion, called Cliveden, where the 40th Regiment (300 strong) was posted. Unable to stop the American advance, more than half of the 40th Regiment retreated with the light infantry back towards the main British camp.[8]

About 100 soldiers of the 40th Regiment, however, including their commander, Lieutenant Colonel Thomas Musgrave, barricaded themselves inside Cliveden and refused to surrender after the Americans surrounded the building.[9]

General Washington, who had accompanied General Sullivan's wing in the attack, came upon the scene and considered bypassing the obstinate enemy in the mansion, but

---

[7] McGuire, *The Philadelphia Campaign: Germantown and the Roads to Valley Forge*, Vol. 2, 67
[8] Ibid., 68 , 70, 76-77, 80-81
[9] Ibid., 81, 83, 85

General Knox argued that it would be dangerous to leave them in the rear and convinced Washington to order an attack.[10]

Instead of pressing forward with the rest of General Sullivan's wing, a significant number of Sullivan's troops focused their attention and efforts on dislodging the 100 British troops from Cliveden. Efforts to blast the British out with cannon, storm the mansion with infantry, and even burn the building, all failed. The 40th Regiment refused to budge and in doing so, they helped undermine the American attack.[11]

It was during these efforts to capture Cliveden that General Greene's troops arrived on the scene, forty minutes behind schedule. Part of General Stephen's division, on Greene's right, was drawn to the fighting at Clivedon, where they added to the roar of battle, but the rest of Stephen's division marched past with General Greene's wing.[12]

General Wayne, who had earlier advanced several hundred yards past Cliveden with Sullivan's wing, heard intense fighting to his rear and became worried that the enemy had somehow gotten behind him through the fog and smoke. He turned his brigade around and marched back towards Cliveden to investigate.[13] To his front appeared a long line of dark figures, mostly obscured by the thick fog. Suddenly a volley erupted from this line, blasting the Pennsylvanians. Those of General Wayne's troops who didn't panic and break naturally returned fire, striking some of General Stephen's Virginians.[14] A tragic case of friendly fire had occurred and many of the

---

[10] McGuire, *The Philadelphia Campaign: Germantown and the Roads to Valley Forge,* Vol. 2, 87
[11] Ibid., 88-91
[12] Ibid., 94-95
[13] Ibid., 97
[14] Ibid., 99

Pennsylvanians assumed they had been flanked by the enemy. As a result, General Wayne's brigade lost its order and fled.[15]

Although the mishap between the Virginians and Pennsylvanians blunted the momentum of Washington's attack, the bulk of General Greene's troops further to the left, including Major Campbell and the 13th Virginians with General Muhlenberg's brigade, were unaware of the mistake and pressed forward to engage the British 1st Light Infantry Battalion.

Sixteen year old Joseph Plum Martin was with the Connecticut troops who fought alongside the Virginians and recalled that

> *The enemy were driven quite through their camp. They left their kettles, in which they were cooking their breakfast, on the fires, and some of their garments were lying on the ground, which the owners had not time to put on.*[16]

General Greene's troops continued forward, but the disarray of Sullivan's right wing left Greene's right flank vulnerable. General Muhlenberg's 9th Virginia Regiment probably advanced the furthest of any American unit, but in doing so, they soon found themselves swarmed upon by British reinforcements who encircled them.[17] With no support on their flanks, the surrounded 9th Virginians had no choice

---

[15] Ibid.
[16] Joseph Plum Martin, *Private Yankee Doolittle: Being a Narrative of Some of the Adventures, Dangers and Sufferings of a Revolutionary Soldier*, (Eastern Acorn Press, 1998), 73
    Originally published in 1840.
[17] McGuire, *The Philadelphia Campaign: Germantown and the Roads to Valley Forge*, Vol. 2, 114-115

but to surrender.[18] Recognizing that the situation was deteriorating precipitously, General Greene ordered his wing to retreat before they too were cut off.[19]

General Washington was stunned at these developments. In a candid letter to his brother John Augustine two weeks after the battle, Washington admitted that he was still at a loss to identify the cause of their loss at Germantown.

> *After they* [the British] *had crossed* [into Philadelphia] *we took the first favourable opportunity of attacking them – This we attempted by a Nights March of fourteen Miles to surprise them (which we effectually did) so far as reaching their Guards before they had notice of our coming, and but for a thick Fog rendered so infinitely dark at times, as not to distinguish friend from Foe, at the distance of 30 Yards, we should, I believe, have made a decisive & glorious day of it.*[20]

General Washington continued.

> *But Providence – or some unaccountable something, designd it otherwise; for after we had driven the Enemy a Mile or two, after they were in the utmost confusion, and flying before us in most places, after we were upon the point (as it appeard to every body) of grasping a compleat Victory, our own Troops took fright & fled with precipitation and disorder. How to*

---

[18] Ibid., 115
[19] Ibid., 115-116
[20] Chase and Lengel, eds., "General Washington to John Augustine Washington, October 18, 1777," *The Papers of George Washington, Revolutionary Series*, Vol. 11, 551

> *account for this I know not, unless, as I before observ'd, the Fog represented their own Friends to them for a Reinforcement of the Enemy as we attacked in different Quarters at the same time, & were about closing the Wings of our Army when this happened.*[21]

General Washington added that the fighting lasted nearly three hours during which many of his troops expended all of their ammunition.[22] With much of his army in disarray, General Washington ordered his men to return to their old encampment at Pennibackers Mill (about 20 miles from Philadelphia) where they could treat the wounded and reorganize themselves. Fortunately, the British, who may have felt fortunate themselves to have survived Washington's surprise attack, did not aggressively pursue.

Accounts of the performance of the 13th Virginia in the battle varied. General Adam Stephen noted in a long letter to General Washington that Colonel Russell and Major Campbell [of the 13th Virginia], *"behaved Gallantly during the Action."*[23] However, Lieutenant James McMichael, who fought with a Pennsylvania regiment attached to General Muhlenberg's brigade, noted in his diary that, *"The cowardice of the 13th Virginia regiment gave the enemy an opportunity of coming around our left flank."*[24] With generalized

---

[21] Chase and Lengel, eds., "General Washington to John Augustine Washington, October 18, 1777," *The Papers of George Washington, Revolutionary Series*, Vol. 11, 551

[22] Ibid.

[23] Chase and Lengel, eds., "Major Stephen to General Washington, October 9, 1777," *The Papers of George Washington*, Vol. 11, 468-469

[24] James McMichael, "October 4, 1777 entry, Diary of Lieutenant James McMichael, of the Pennsylvania Line, 1776-1778," *The Pennsylvania Magazine of History and Biography*, Vol. 16, No. 2, 153

observations like these, it is difficult to determine with any specificity the actions Major Campbell or the men of the 13th Virginia took in the battle. All we can really determine is that they fought with the rest of General Muhlenberg's brigade in the left wing of the American attack.

American losses at Germantown were significant, as was the drop in morale among Washington's troops. His army needed rest and reinforcements, and it fortunately received both in the weeks following Germantown.

Seemingly content with his capture of Philadelphia, General Howe and the bulk of his army was relatively inactive after Germantown. There was some activity downriver from Philadelphia that involved the British navy and a portion of Howe's troops (both of who worked to capture American forts that obstructed passage of the river) but military activity between the main armies of Howe and Washington subsided considerably in the weeks following Germantown.

This was very fortunate for the Americans as many of Washington's troops were in poor condition, particularly in regards to clothing.[25] Much needed reinforcements from the victorious American northern army at Saratoga arrived in November, lifting American morale with their presence and details of their victory over the British in New York.

General Washington used the lull in activity after Germantown to address several disciplinary issues among his general officers. Accusations of misconduct in some form during the recent campaign were leveled against Generals Sullivan, Maxwell, Wayne, and Stephen. Boards of inquiry

---

[25] Chase and Lengel, eds., "General Washington to John Hancock, October 13-14, 1777, Enclosed Return," *The Papers of George Washington, Revolutionary Series*, Vol. 11, 500

and courts martial addressed the charges and found only one senior officer guilty of significant wrongdoing. General Adam Stephen was convicted of unofficerlike behavior during the retreat from Germantown and of also being too often intoxicated while in the service, *"to the prejudice of good order and military discipline."*[26] He was dismissed from the army as a result.

British efforts to open navigation of the Delaware River all the way to Philadelphia succeeded in mid-November with the fall of two American forts that had obstructed passage. In December, a large part of the British army marched out of Philadelphia towards Washington's army, which was encamped in the hills of Whitemarsh, north of the city. A heated, but limited, engagement occurred of little consequence (except of course to those involved) and General Howe returned to Philadelphia with his troops for the rest of the winter.

General Washington moved his army west, to Valley Forge, and ordered his troops to construct log huts and earthworks. Washington was determined to keep his army together and remain a threat, albeit from 25 miles away, to General Howe and his army. Whether he was able to accomplish either goal remained to be seen.

---

[26] Frank E. Grizzard, Jr., ed., "General Orders, November 20, 1777," *The Papers of George Washington, Revolutionary War Series,* Vol. 12, (University Press of Virginia, 2002), 327-328

Valley Forge

The condition of the American army when they arrived at Valley Forge was truly deplorable. Many of the men were unfit for duty because of a lack of clothing and shoes, a significant problem with winter upon them. An even larger number of troops were too ill to remain with the army, especially since their winter quarters had yet to be built. The men needed fires for warmth and tents would not do, so Washington ordered the troops to build huts as fast as they could.[27] Exhausted and hungry, those capable set to work, a chore that took weeks to complete. The troops also had to work on earthworks, but the huts came first.

Major Campbell and the 13th Virginia numbered less than 70 men in camp at the end of December, about 10% of its authorized strength.[28] Eighty men were away from Valley Forge due to illness and another 25 were on command (perhaps detached to Colonel Morgan's Rifle Corps or assigned to assist several officers.[29] There was also the detached portion of the regiment still at Fort Pitt; approximately three companies of over 100 men, that were not included in the regiment's troop return at Valley Forge.[30]

Lieutenant Colonel John Gibson was with those men and actually commanded the entire garrison at Fort Pitt during part

---

[27] Grizzard, Jr., ed., "General Orders, December 18, 1777," *The Papers of George Washington, Revolutionary War Series,* Vol. 12, 627
[28] Lesser, ed., "A General Return of the Continental Army…December 31, 1777," *The Sinews of Independence,* 54
[29] Ibid.
[30] Grizzard, Jr., ed., "Colonel John Gibson to General Washington, December 5, 1777," *The Papers of George Washington, Revolutionary War Series,* Vol. 12, 562-563

of the winter of 1777-78.[31] His promotion to colonel of the 6th Virginia Regiment in April of 1778, however, complicated matters, for his frontier experience and leadership made him an irreplaceable presence at Fort Pitt, yet his new command was with General Washington at Valley Forge.[32]

Colonel Russell, Major Campbell, and the handful of men of the 13th Virginia at Valley Forge who were still able to perform duty (which fell to only 27 officers and men in March) suffered through the difficult winter with the rest of General Washington's army.[33]

In late February, Colonel Russell wrote to General Washington to inquire whether information provided by Major Campbell was correct.

> *I am happy to be inform'd by Major Campbell, that your Excellency intends shortly to have the divided and disagreeable situation of the 13th Virginia Regiment laid before Congress; that thereby that part of the Regiment here, and those over the Mountain at Fort Pitt may be join'd together, and act accordingly at such place as your Excellency and Congress may think proper to direct.* [34]

---

[31] Edward G. Lengel, ed., "General Washington to Colonel John Gibson, December 29, 1777," *The Papers of George Washington*, Vol. 13, (Charlottesville: University of Virginia Press, 2003), 41-42

[32] David R. Hoth, ed., "General Orders, April 25, 1778," *The Papers of George Washington*, Vol. 14, (Charlottesville: The University of Virginia Press, 2004), 617

[33] Lesser, ed., "Monthly Return of the Continental Forces Under the Immediate Command of…General Washington…for March 1778," *The Sinews of Independence*, 60

[34] Lengel, ed., "Colonel Russell to General Washington, February 24, 1778," *The Papers of George Washington*, Vol. 13, 656-657

How Major Campbell came upon such information is a mystery, but it may have been as simple as a dinner conversation with the General as Washington frequently invited junior officers to dine with him as a way to maintain morale.

However Major Campbell came upon the information, it was indeed General Washington's desire to unite the 13th Virginia. He discussed the matter with Henry Laurens, the President of the Congress, several days later in a letter.

> *I am under some embarrassment respecting the 13th Virginia Regiment. It was raised on the West side of the Alleghaney and towards Pittsburg with assurances from the Officers, it is said, that the Men would not be drawn from that Quarter. This circumstance, added to the disturbances by the Indians & the exposed situation of their families, has been the cause of great desertions, and is at present the source of much uneasiness; and the more so as part of the Regiment was never marched from thence. I think the whole should be united, either here or there, and wish Congress to direct me upon the subject.*[35]

Colonel Russell had requested in his letter to Washington that Major Campbell be granted a leave of absence to wait on Congress (in York, Pennsylvania) to have the situation of the 13th Virginia adjusted.[36] This was apparently granted, for a month later Major Campbell delivered a letter to General

---

[35] Lengel, ed., "General Washington to Henry Laurens, February 27, 1778," *The Papers of George Washington*, Vol. 13, 686-687.

[36] Lengel, ed., "Colonel Russell to General Washington, February 24, 1778," *The Papers of George Washington*, Vol. 13, 656-657.

Washington from General Horatio Gates, who was then in York. In his reply to Gates, Washington reported that he was unable to send the few troops of the 13th Virginia at Valley Forge to Fort Pitt because the army's troop strength was desperately reduced by inoculations (for small pox). General Washington did agree, however, to send Colonel Russell to Fort Pitt to, *"collect and take the command of by far the greatest part of the Regiment who are now stragling about that Country."*[37] Washington added that,

> *Major Campbell informs me that there ought to be four hundred Men there. There are not above one hundred* [of the 13th Virginia] *here sick and well.*[38]

Major Campbell's estimate of 400 men of the 13th Virginia out west was likely an exaggeration. Half that number would have been an impressive turnout, given the difficult circumstances American forces faced both in the east and west in March 1778.

The situation improved considerably for the Americans at Valley Forge when news arrived in May of a new alliance with France. Many were confident that French assistance would turn the tide and help make short work of driving the British from North America.

General Washington's troop strength also improved considerably with the onset of spring. The 13th Virginia tripled its effective strength at Valley Forge, admittedly still small, from 27 officers and men fit for duty in March to 75 in

---

[37] Hoth, ed., "General Washington to General Gates, March 25, 1778," *The Papers of George Washington*, Vol. 14, 304
[38] Ibid.

May.[39] General Washington's army experienced similar growth, swelling from 7,316 effective officers and men in March to 15,061 in May.[40]

Such growth allowed Washington to finally send the troops of the 13th Virginia that were still at Valley Forge westward under Major Campbell.

> *You are to march immediately with the thirteenth Virginia Regiment to York Town in Pennsylvania, going through Lancaster and collecting from the Hospitals there and at other places all the convalescents belonging to the said Regiment who are able to proceed. You will also remain with the Regiment after it arrives at Yorktown till it receives further orders respecting it's destination;*[41]

General Washington apparently did not intend to part with Major Campbell, however, for he included a surprising addition to the end of his orders.

> *When that is done, and the Regiment begins it's march from thence, you are to return immediately and join this Army.*[42]

---

[39] Lesser, ed., "Monthly Return of the Continental Army…May 30, 1778," *The Sinews of Independence,* 68

[40] Lesser, ed., "Monthly Return of the Continental Forces Under the Immediate Command of…General Washington…for March 1778," and "Monthly Return of the Continental Army…May 30, 1778," *The Sinews of Independence,* 61, 69

[41] Edward G. Lengel, ed., "General Washington to Major Richard Campbell, May 24, 1778," *The Papers of George Washington,* Vol. 15, (Charlottesville: University of Virginia Press, 2006), 208

[42] Ibid.

Major Campbell was not the only officer of the 13th Virginia to be surprised by General Washington in May. Just a few days after he issued his orders to Campbell, Washington ordered Colonel John Gibson of the 6th Virginia and Colonel William Russell of the 13th Virginia to temporarily trade regiments.[43] Washington included his rational for replacing Russell (who was already at Fort Pitt) with Gibson (who had spent the winter there but was now at Valley Forge) in a letter to Henry Laurens, the President of Congress.

> *Lt. Colo. John Gibson of the 6th Virginia Regiment, who, from his knowledge of the Western Country and Indian Nations and language, is ordered to repair to Pitsburg will have the honor of delivering you this.*[44]

General Washington gave a similar explanation to Colonel Russell.

> *The particular situation of Indian Affairs to the Westward rendering it necessary to send up Officers acquainted with their language, customs and Country, I have...ordered Colo.* [John] *Gibson to Pitts Burgh with Brig. Genl. McIntosh.*[45]

General Washington explained that since there were only two regiments assigned to Fort Pitt (the 13th VA and 8th PA) but three colonels, he had decided to recall Colonel Russell to

---

[43] Lengel, ed., "General Washington to Colonel Russell, May 28, 1778," *The Papers of George Washington*, Vol. 15, 249

[44] .Lengel, ed., "General Washington to Henry Laurens, May 28, 1778," *The Papers of George Washington*, Vol. 15, 247

[45] Lengel, ed., "General Washington to Colonel Russell, May 28, 1778," *The Papers of George Washington*, Vol. 15, 249

the main army to command Colonel Gibson's 6th Virginia. Washington assured Russell that, *"My only reason for making this temporary change is, that the nature of the service calls for an Officer accustomed to the management of Indians, and you can be more usefully employed here."*[46]

Two weeks earlier General Washington had appointed General Lachlan McIntosh of Georgia to command the western department, including the troops at Fort Pitt. He was ordered to wait on Congress at York, Pennsylvania for further orders.[47] McIntosh was still in York in early June when Major Campbell arrived with the 13th Virginia and he used Campbell to convey a dispatch back to General Washington.

> *There are the most distressing Accounts from the frontier Settlements by the Inroads & Barbarity of the Savages, the Militia are dispirited & removing, and Genl Hand in a very disagreeable Situation, with about 100 Men at Fort Pitt, unable to give them any assistance....*[48]

General McIntosh urged that the continental troops at York, the 13th Virginia and 8th Pennsylvania, be sent immediately with him to Fort Pitt. He added a further request, the return of Major Campbell to the 13th Virginia.

---

[46] Lengel, ed., "General Washington to Colonel Russell, May 28, 1778," *The Papers of George Washington*, Vol. 15, 249
[47] Lengel, ed., "General Washington to Henry Laurens, May 12, 1778," *The Papers of George Washington*, Vol. 15, 108
[48] Lengel, ed., "General McIntosh to General Washington, June 7, 1778," *The Papers of George Washington*, Vol. 15, 345

> *I Submit to Your Excellency, if it will not be Necessary to Send the bearer Major Campbell back to me again either in the Capacity he is now in, or as Lieut. Colonel if he is entitled to it, as the 13th Regiment has no other Field Officer but Colo. Russell. I have reason to think it would not be disagreeable to himself.*[49]

A sort of tug of war appears to have commenced over Major Campbell, who delivered McIntosh's request to Washington in mid-June.

General Washington agreed to General McIntosh's request and sent Major Campbell straight back to York with a message for Congress. It read:

> *Major Campbell of the 13th Virginia Regiment will have the Honor of presenting you with this. He is now on his way at the earnest solicitation of General McIntosh to serve in the Western department and waites on Congress to obtain, if they shall think proper, a Commission for a Lieutenant Colonelcy in the Virginia Line, to which he has been intitled in the ordinary course, since the 20th of February last.*[50]

General Washington held Campbell in high regard, adding that,

---

[49] Lengel, ed., "General McIntosh to General Washington, June 7, 1778," *The Papers of George Washington*, Vol. 15, 345

[50] Lengel, ed., "General Washington to Henry Laurens, June 10, 1778," *The Papers of George Washington*, Vol. 15, 372-373

> *The Major sustains the character of a good and brave Officer and has behaved as such during his service. He is the more desirous of getting a Commission at this time, as otherwise he may be commanded by the Lieutenant Colonels to be, or who are appointed to the two new Regiments, lately ordered to be raised in that Quarter. I do not know the particular Regiment to which he should be affixed, therefore, if he obtains a Commission it may be left blank in this instance.*[51]

Although General Washington had expressed his view that Major Campbell was entitled to a promotion, there were several "older" majors in the Virginia continental line ahead of Campbell, so his promotion to Lieutenant Colonel would once again create dissention among some of his fellow officers. Henry Laurens revealed the solution that Congress came up with in his reply to General Washington.

> *Major Campbell's new Commission is a Brevet Lt. Colonel, this Rank to have effect only in the Western department not to affect any Officer in the Virginia line nor to entitle him to any other pay than that of Major the Rank he held previous to his appointment to rank from 20th February 1778.*[52]

Although it is likely Lieutenant Colonel Campbell found this arrangement less than satisfactory, it relieved his concern

---

[51] Lengel, ed., "General Washington to Henry Laurens, June 10, 1778," *The Papers of George Washington*, Vol. 15, 372-373
[52] Lengel, ed., "Henry Laurens to General Washington, June 20, 1778," *The Papers of George Washington*, Vol. 15, 482

of being placed under the command of younger lieutenant colonels of the new western regiments that Congress had authorized and that were then being raised (ever so slowly), to join the forces already at Fort Pitt. Lieutenant Colonel Campbell thus rode west with General McIntosh and the 13th Virginia to join the rest of the regiment at Fort Pitt.

Chapter Four

To chastise and terrify the savages, and to check their ravages on the frontier....

1778-1780

Lieutenant Colonel Campbell arrived at Fort Pitt with General McIntosh in early August.[1] Congress had intended General McIntosh to lead an expedition against the important British post at Detroit, but while McIntosh and Campbell made their way to Fort Pitt, Congress abandoned this idea and instead instructed General McIntosh to lead an expedition, *"to destroy such towns of the hostile tribes of Indians as he...shall think will most effectively tend to chastise and terrify the savages, and to check their ravages on the frontier...."*[2]

Congress instructed General McIntosh to raise a force of 1,500 continental and militia troops to accomplish this new mission.[3] Obtaining enough food for the troops and forage for the horses that were needed to transport all of the supplies for such a force proved immensely difficult and McIntosh was unable to depart from Fort Pitt until late October.[4]

---

[1] Louise P. Kellogg, ed., "General Edward Hand to Mrs. Hand, August 6, 1778," *Frontier Advance on the Upper Ohio, 1778-79*, (Madison, WI : Wisconsin Historical Society, 1916), 125
[2] Ford., ed., Congressional Resolution, July 25, 1778," *Journals of the Continental Congress,* Vol. 11, 720
[3] Ibid.
[4] Kellogg, ed., "General McIntosh to Colonel Steel, October 19, 1778," and "General McIntosh to Colonel John Campbell, October 25, 1778," *Frontier Advance on the Upper Ohio, 1778-79,* 145-146, 148-149

About 30 miles down the Ohio River from Fort Pitt, General McIntosh halted and ordered the construction of a fort on the north bank of the river (dubbed Fort McIntosh) to serve as a supply depot for his expedition.[5] McIntosh and most of his troops resumed their march west after a week long halt, leaving Lieutenant Colonel Campbell and 150 men to finish the fort and garrison it. More importantly, Campbell was instructed to collect food and forage for the expedition as fast as possible.[6]

> *You are Immediately to take charge and Command of this Post with all the Troops left here until further orders. You are to get the Fort Finished as soon as possible.... As the want of our Stores and Provisions has detained me so long here, and obliges me late as it is now to proceed only with part of the army, you are therefore to exert your utmost endevours in Collecting them with all possible dispatch into this Fort.... Flour, Forage, Salt, and Whiskey are the principle things we are in need of.*[7]

Lieutenant Colonel Campbell struggled mightily to fulfill his instructions, but malnourished horses (due to overwork and the lack of forage) and obstinate quarter masters (who did not send the supplies they promised to send), frustrated his efforts. Campbell informed General McIntosh a week after McIntosh's departure that,

---

[5] Kellogg, ed., *Frontier Advance on the Upper Ohio, 1778-79*, 23
[6] Ibid., and "General McIntosh to Colonel Campbell, November 3, 1778," *Frontier Advance on the Upper Ohio, 1778-79*, 164
[7] Ibid.

> *I am doing every thing I possibly can towards getting forage to this place.... I am afraid I shall be under the disagreeable Necessity of differing with...all the [Quarter Masters]. I have one now under arrest.*[8]

General McIntosh was equally frustrated about the condition of his pack horses, complaining to Lieutenant Colonel Campbell ten days into his march that, *"I am not 50 miles from your fort yet owing to the scandalous Pack Horses that were imposed on me...."*[9] In an earlier letter to Campbell, General McIntosh lamented that many of his pack horses could only manage 4 or 5 miles a day with only 100 pound loads of provisions and supplies.[10]

Lieutenant Colonel Campbell vigorously pressed those tasked with supplying the army and in doing so, ruffled a few feathers. Colonel Archibald Steel was one such supplier who expressed his displeasure with the tone of Campbell's letters.

> *The reason for my not making you a Return of my Stores before this time,* [wrote Steel to Campbell] *is...there hath been such Confusion in every Department.... You seem to be particular in demanding a Just Return. Do you know that ever I made a false one? I must tell you Sir, it appears to me in your letters you are not acquainted with my*

---

[8] Kellogg, ed., "Colonel Campbell to General McIntosh, November 10, 1778," *Frontier Advance on the Upper Ohio, 1778-79,* 169

[9] Kellogg, ed., "General McIntosh to Colonel Campbell, November 13, 1778," *Frontier Advance on the Upper Ohio, 1778-79,* 172

[10] Kellogg, ed., "General McIntosh to Colonel Campbell, November 7, 1778," *Frontier Advance on the Upper Ohio, 1778-79,* 167-168

> *business in the Country, if you do you mean to insult me.*[11]

Lieutenant Colonel Campbell's efforts produced results, and two weeks after McIntosh's departure, Campbell informed McIntosh that,

> *It appears I have plenty of forage Coming in both by land and water. I expect to have 1,000 or 1,500 Bushels at this Spot in a few days, and shall be able to keep my Waggon Horses going, and hope to have that much always by me.*[12]

Not all of Campbell's news was good, however. He estimated that there was only a 62 day supply of flour for the army, *"on this side of the Allegany Mountains,"* and little chance to obtain more before spring.[13] There was also not enough salt available for both McIntosh's troops and those with Campbell at Fort McIntosh to allow both groups to butcher and salt the cattle with the army.[14]

By early December, General McIntosh had reached the Tuscarawas River, about 70 miles west of Fort McIntosh.[15] With most of the militia demanding their release, he was unable to march any further west. Instead, he built another fort, dubbed Fort Laurens, with barracks to hold 200 men.

---

[11] Kellogg, ed., "Colonel Archibald Steel to Colonel Campbell, November 16-17, 1778," *Frontier Advance on the Upper Ohio, 1778-79*, 173

[12] Kellogg, ed., "Colonel Campbell to General McIntosh, November 18, 1778," *Frontier Advance on the Upper Ohio, 1778-79*, 174

[13] Ibid.

[14] Ibid.

[15] Kellogg, ed., "General McIntosh to Colonel Fleming, December 7, 1778," *Frontier Advance on the Upper Ohio, 1778-79*, 183-184

McIntosh hoped the presence of such a garrison, *"will Secure the peace on our Frontiers in this quarter at least."*[16]

Colonel John Gibson commanded a garrison of 150 troops of the 13th Virginia at Fort Laurens; they were to remain there over the winter.[17] General McIntosh led the rest of his force eastward, back to Fort Pitt, where he dismissed what remained of the militia (those that had not departed on their own on the way back) and ordered the remaining continental troops to garrison Fort Pitt and several small forts in the area.[18]

Lieutenant Colonel Campbell relinquished command of Fort McIntosh to Colonel Daniel Brodhead of the 8th Pennsylvania Regiment at some point in January.[19] It is difficult to determine Richard Campbell's activities over the next few months of 1779. Outranked by several officers who had returned from General McIntosh's expedition, he likely served as a subordinate officer at one or several of the frontier forts. It is possible, however, that he was granted a furlough to visit his family in Virginia. The documentary evidence is scant on his actions between January and March of 1779.

The situation for Campbell's regimental commander, Colonel John Gibson, was much clearer and unfortunately, dire. Short on provisions and separated by 70 miles from his nearest support at Fort McIntosh, Gibson and his men held tight at Fort Laurens. Rumors of an impending Indian attack kept the garrison on edge and yet, when the attack came in late February, it caught the garrison by surprise. General

---

[16] Ibid.
[17] Kellogg, ed., *Frontier Advance on the Upper Ohio, 1778-79*, 24
[18] Kellogg, ed., "General McIntosh to Board of War, January 11, 1779," *Frontier Advance on the Upper Ohio, 1778-79*, 197-198
[19] Kellogg, ed., "Colonel George Morgan to Colonel Broadhead, January 31, 1779," *Frontier Advance on the Upper Ohio, 1778-79*, 216

McIntosh relayed the details of the attack to General Washington.

> *A waggoner who was sent out of the fort for the horses to draw wood, and 18 men to guard him, were fired upon, and all killed and scalped in sight of the fort.*[20]

The ambush marked the commencement of a four week siege upon Fort Laurens, a siege that took the garrison to the brink of starvation. One of Colonel Gibson's men recalled that

> *The siege lasted some 4 weeks, provisions exhausted: finally for 3 or 4 days had to live on half a biscuit a day – then, the last two days washed their moccasons and broiled them for food, and broiled strips of old dried hides.*[21]

Fortunately for Colonel Gibson and his garrison at Fort Laurens, General McIntosh arrived with 500 men and provisions to relieve the fort in mid-March.[22] They did not have to fight their way there as expected because the Indians surrounding Fort Laurens had lifted the siege just before they arrived. Word of the capture of British governor Henry

---

[20] Philander D. Chase and William M. Ferraro, eds., "General McIntosh to General Washington, March 12, 1779," *The Papers of George Washington,* Vol. 19, (Charlottesville : University Press of Virginia, 2009), 453

[21] Kellogg, ed., "Recollections of Benjamin Biggs," *Frontier Advance on the Upper Ohio, 1778-79,* 256-257

[22] Chase and Ferraro, eds., "General McIntosh to General Washington, March 19, 1779," *The Papers of George Washington,* Vol. 19, 531

Hamilton at Vincennes by George Rogers Clark shook had demoralized the Indians and the siege was lifted as a result.[23]

General McIntosh, who was not aware that his request to be recalled had been granted by Congress weeks earlier, proposed to push most of his force further west, but this was universally opposed by the officers with him, including Lieutenant Colonel Campbell, who argued that the difficult terrain and conditions they would encounter in early spring as well as the lack of the supplies would not allow such a movement.[24] McIntosh thus left Major Frederick Vernon and a new detachment of approximately 100 men to garrison Fort Laurens and returned with the rest of his troops to Fort Pitt where he learned that he had been relieved.[25] Colonel Daniel Brodhead assumed command of the American forces in the region.

New Arrangement of the Virginia Line

Although the conduct of the war had slowed considerably in the east following the Battle of Monmouth in June of 1778, General Washington had remained active with his army. In the fall of 1778 he consolidated several Virginia regiments and rearranged the entire Virginia line. The 13th Virginia Regiment was re-designated the 9th Virginia Regiment (although correspondence from the western department

---

[23] Kellogg, ed., *Frontier Advance on the Upper Ohio, 1778-79*, 25
[24] Chase and Ferraro, eds., "General McIntosh to General Washington, April 3, 1779," *The Papers of George Washington*, Vol. 19, 724-725 and Edward G. Lengel, ed., "General McIntosh to General Washington, May 3, 1779," *The Papers of George Washington*, Vol. 20, (Charlottesville : University of Virginia Press, 2010), 312
[25] Ibid.

continued to refer to the unit as the 13th Virginia well into 1779). Lieutenant Colonel Campbell continued in service with the regiment and awaited orders from Colonel Brodhead, who in turn awaited instructions from General Washington.

The American commander-in-chief had settled upon a plan in the spring of 1779 to strike hard at the Iroquois Indians in Pennsylvania and western New York. He hoped to end the constant attacks upon the frontier settlers of that region and detached a significant portion of his army to do so.

Colonel Brodhead was eager to participate, but logistical challenges of launching a secondary offensive from Fort Pitt convinced General Washington that it was best to maintain a defensive posture in the west.[26] Brodhead was ordered to retain Fort Laurens (which he had long wanted to abandon) as well as most of the other forts in the region.

In mid-June, Lieutenant Colonel Campbell was ordered to march with a relief detachment to Fort Laurens and assume command of the fort, garrisoning it with 75 men.[27] He and his men had garrisoned the fort for about a month when new orders arrived from Colonel Brodhead. He had received permission from General Washington to conduct an expedition from Fort Pitt up the Allegheny River against the Mingo Indians to support Washington's main thrust against the Iroquois to the east.[28] Colonel Broadhead seized this

---

[26] Lengel, ed., "General Washington to Colonel Brodhead, May 3, 1779," *The Papers of George Washington*, Vol. 20, 299

[27] Kellogg, ed., "Colonel Daniel Brodhead's Orders, June 14, 1779," *Frontier Advance on the Upper Ohio, 1778-79*, 364

[28] William M. Ferraro, ed., "General Washington to Colonel Brodhead, June 23, 1779," *The Papers of George Washington*, Vol. 21, (Charlottesville : University of Virginia Press, 2012), 216-217

opportunity to take the offensive and moved to consolidate his forces. He informed Lieutenant Colonel Campbell that

> *Fort Laurens will be evacuated as soon as horses can be sent out to bring in the stores – but this must be kept a profound secret; and as your post may again be occasionally occupied, the works are not to be demolished by our troops.*[29]

Lieutenant Colonel Campbell apparently questioned the wisdom of evacuating Fort Laurens and wrote to Colonel Brodhead with his objections. Brodhead was furious at Campbell's resistance and sent a stinging reply.

> *I have received your very extraordinary letter.... How an officer, who has served so long as you mention should have misconceived language and circumstances so plain as was contained in my Letter, and the arrival of Captain Harrison with the Pack Horses, I am at a loss to conceive. However, I will now give it more plain if possible.*
> *Sir, I mean as I said before that Fort* [Laurens] *must be evacuated, and as Captain Harrison told you, he was to bring off the stores on the Pack Horses, under his escort and they are not to be slaughtered.*[30]

---

[29] Kellogg, ed., "Colonel Brodhead to Colonel Campbell, July 16, 1779," *Frontier Advance on the Upper Ohio, 1778-79,* 389

[30] Samuel Hazard, ed., "Colonel Brodhead to Lieutenant Colonel Campbell, July 30th, 1779," *Pennsylvania Archives,* Series 1, Vol. 12, (Philadelphia : Joseph Severns & Co., 1856), 141

Lieutenant Colonel Campbell and his garrison evacuated Fort Laurens in early August and proceeded to Fort Pitt.[31] Colonel Brodhead waited impatiently and sent a follow up note to Campbell to hurry him along.

> *Your obstinacy has already delayed the expedition I informed you of, & I expect, unless this meets you near at hand, to march without your Garrison.*[32]

Campbell and his men reached Fort Pitt on August 7th and then marched north with Colonel Brodhead's force, approximately 600 strong, when Brodhead commenced his expedition on August 11th.[33] His objective was to destroy as many hostile Indian towns and their crops, mostly corn, as he could in the one month he figured his own supplies would last.[34]

Brodhead reported to General Washington upon his return to Fort Pitt in mid-September that his expedition destroyed 500 acres of corn and other crops as well as several Indian towns, all at very little loss, albeit some discomfort, to his men.[35] He also lavished praise on his officers and men in his letter to Washington.

---

[31] Kellogg, ed., "Recollections of Henry Jolly," *Frontier Advance on the Upper Ohio, 1778-79*, 257

[32] Hazard, ed., "Colonel Brodhead to Lieutenant Colonel Campbell, August 7th, 1779," *Pennsylvania Archives*, Series 1, Vol. 12, 154

[33] Benjamin Huggins, ed., "Colonel Brodhead to General Washington, September 16-24, 1779," *The Papers of George Washington*, Vol. 22, (Charlottesville : University of Virginia Press, 2013), 433

[34] Huggins, ed., "Colonel Brodhead to General Washington, September 16-24, 1779," *The Papers of George Washington*, Vol. 22, 433

[35] Ibid., 435

> *Too much praise cannot be given to both Officers & Soldiers of every Corps during the whole expedition their perseverance & zeal during the whole march thro' a Country too inaccessible to be described can scarcely be equaled in history, notwithstanding many of them returned barefooted & (almost) naked they disdained to complain & to my great mortification I have neither Shoes, Shirts, Blankets, Hats, Stockings, nor leggings to relieve their necessities.*[36]

Brodhead believed his successful expedition ensured that, "*The frontier of our State will enjoy a perfect tranquility*;" yet, he was also ready to press westward to Detroit.[37] Alas, General Washington refused to authorize such a move so Colonel Brodhead and the troops of the western department settled down for another winter on the frontier.

Lieutenant Colonel Campbell's activities in October and November 1779 are somewhat of a mystery. He could very well have been posted at Fort Pitt or some other garrison, or perhaps he was sent back home to recruit. Correspondence from Colonel Brodhead to Major Richard Taylor of the 9th Virginia (who was posted at Fort McIntosh) suggests that Lieutenant Colonel Campbell may have indeed been sent briefly to Virginia to collect reinforcements. Brodhead informed Taylor in mid-December that

---

[36] Huggins, ed., "Colonel Brodhead to General Washington, September 16-24, 1779," *The Papers of George Washington*, Vol. 22, 435.

[37] Hazard, ed., "Colonel Brodhead to Governor Reed, October 9, 1779," *Pennsylvania Archives*, Series 1, Vol. 12, 163-164.

> *Col. Campbell waits a few days at this place,* [Fort Pitt] *at my insistence; as soon as I receive another express from the Commander in Chief I shall determine how to dispose of the Troops.*[38]

Colonel Brodhead was waiting for General Washington's permission to stage a winter expedition against Detroit, something Brodhead had strongly hinted at a month earlier.[39] While General Washington did not approve of a strike against Detroit, he did give Brodhead permission, *"To act against hostile Indians in such incursions as your circumstances will admit."*[40] As hostile Indian activity had largely subsided, there was little for Colonel Brodhead and his men to do but maintain the several forts that guarded the western frontier.

Major Taylor, at Fort McIntosh, apparently desired that Lieutenant Colonel Campbell replace him as commander of the garrison. He was informed by Colonel Brodhead on December 19th, that for the time being, that wasn't possible.

> *Col. Campbell is very ill at present and it is likely he cannot have a speedy recovery, therefore, you must continue a while longer.*[41]

---

[38] Hazard, ed., "Colonel Brodhead to Major Taylor, December 12, 1779," *Pennsylvania Archives,* Series 1, Vol. 12, 197

[39] William M. Ferraro, ed., "Colonel Brodhead to General Washington, November 10, 1779," *The Papers of George Washington*, Vol. 23, (Charlottesville : University of Virginia Press, 2015), 220-221

[40] Ferraro, ed., "General Washington to Colonel Brodhead, November 21, 1779," *The Papers of George Washington*, Vol. 23, 382

[41] Hazard, ed., "Colonel Brodhead to Major Taylor, December 19, 1779," *Pennsylvania Archives,* Series 1, Vol. 12, 200

Campbell may have recovered faster than expected, because Colonel Brodhead informed Major Taylor at the end of the month that Campbell was back on duty.

> *Lieut. Col. Campbell is upon duty here* [Fort Pitt] *& he cannot now relieve you, nor do I think it advisable to give you leave of absence until I receive answers to the letters I have written to Congress, the Commander-in-Chief and the Board of War.*[42]

Many of the troops of Lieutenant Colonel Campbell's 9th Virginia Regiment (originally the 13th Virginia) were approaching the end of their three year enlistments. Colonel Brodhead informed General Washington that over 100 men of the 9th Virginia were expected to leave in February and that there was little hope of replacing them with new recruits.[43] As a commissioned officer, there was no set term of service for Lieutenant Colonel Campbell and he apparently never gave leaving the army a thought.

The officers and men who remained at their posts in the western department settled into a routine that stretched into spring. For Campbell, that routine was altered in April when he led a scouting party down the Ohio River to the mouth of the Muskingum River. We do not know the details of his reconnaissance mission, just that he returned to Fort Pitt by May 18th, 1780 with, *"no late discoveries."*[44]

---

[42] Hazard, ed., "Colonel Brodhead to Major Taylor, December 30, 1779," *Pennsylvania Archives*, Series 1, Vol. 12, 201

[43] Ferraro, ed., "Colonel Brodhead to General Washington, December 13, 1779," *The Papers of George Washington*, Vol. 23, 588-589

[44] Hazard, ed., "Colonel Brodhead to Colonel Pickering, May 18, 1780," *Pennsylvania Archives*, Series 1, Vol. 12, 237

Virginia Line in Disarray 1780

While Lieutenant Colonel Campbell approached his second full year on the frontier and fifth year in the continental army, the war in the east dragged on. French support and involvement in the war, starting in 1778, led the British to abandon Philadelphia only months after they captured it and concentrate their forces around New York City. Washington's success at the Battle of Monmouth in late June of 1778 demonstrated that the American army that emerged out of Valley Forge was a force equal to the British. Several significant, but limited engagements in 1779 at Stony Point and Paulus Hook reinforced this notion.

A new British commander, General Henry Clinton, shifted British attention and effort to the south in late 1778 and a year and a half later that resulted in the greatest military loss of the war for America, the capture of General Benjamin Lincoln's American southern army at Charleston, South Carolina.

The fall of Charleston on May 12th, 1780 shook American morale. It also devastated what was left of the Virginia continental line, most of which had marched south in the winter of 1779-80 to reinforce Charleston. The surrender of the bulk of Virginia's continental line troops, followed two weeks later by the near annihilation of the Virginia continentals that remained under Colonel Abraham Buford at the Waxhaws in South Carolina, left the Virginia continental line in utter disarray.

General Peter Muhlenberg was in Virginia trying to bolster the existing Virginia line when Charleston fell. As the ranking continental officer in the state, he now re-directed his efforts to completely rebuilding the Virginia Line. General

Washington, informed that Virginia intended to draft up to 5,000 troops for 18 month terms of enlistment as continentals (Virginia actually settled on 3,000 troops) instructed General Muhlenberg to rebuild the Virginia line with the handful of officers who had somehow avoided capture at Charleston. Many of these men were in Virginia either sick, recruiting, or on leave, when Charleston fell, and Washington used them to organize seven "new" Virginia regiments that would be manned by the new recruits and draftees.[45]

Lieutenant Colonel Campbell's 9th Virginia Regiment was the lone Virginia regiment of continentals to avoid any loss at Charleston and the Waxhaws. General Washington included the 9th Virginia in his list of seven regiments and as it was still intact, albeit significantly understrength, there was no need to reorganize the 9th Virginia like the other six "new" regiments.

Lieutenant Colonel Campbell, however, after two years at Fort Pitt, desired to leave the frontier. He had actually written to General Washington months earlier, in March, to request a transfer, declaring,

When I Stept forth in the Armey it was my determination to Render my Cuntry Every Service in my Power & wish to be allways where I Could take an Active Part, & as there has Been Officers Ordered from Different Reigts To Command Troops to the Southward I should be Glad to meet with the Same Indulgance if Your Excellency Thought Proper.[46]

---

[45] John C. Fitzpatrick, ed., "General Washington to Major General Gates or Brigadier General Muhlenberg, July 18, 1780," *The Writings of George Washington*, Vol. 19, (Washington, D.C.: U.S. Govt. Printing Officer, 1937), 196-197

[46] Kellogg, "Lt. Col. Campbell to Gen. Washington, March 16, 1780," *Frontier Retreat on the Upper Ohio*, 149-150

Nothing came of Campbell's initial request, but when Major Richard Taylor of the 9th Virginia was promoted to Lieutenant Colonel and transferred to the 11th Virginia -- which was rebuilding at Chesterfield County Courthouse with Virginia's other "new" regiments -- Campbell approached Taylor directly about exchanging units. Taylor apparently preferred to remain on the frontier and was thus amiable to the arrangement. Lieutenant Colonel Campbell asked his old commander, General Muhlenberg to help make the exchange and Muhlenberg wrote to the commander of the American southern army, General Horatio Gates, in late September on Campbell's behalf.

Lieutenant-Colonel Richard Campbell, who has been two campaigns with the 9th regiment at Fort Pitt, requests me to make application to your Excellency for permission to exchange with Lieutenant-Colonel Richard Taylor, who is at present arranged to the 11th regiment, but wishes to exchange it for the 9th. As your Excellency is perfectly acquainted with the character of both the gentlemen, I will only beg leave to say that by the exchange the different genius of both would be suited and the service benefited.[47]

General Gates approved of the arrangement in mid-October but it took several months to implement the exchange during which Campbell remained in the 9th Virginia Regiment.[48]

---

[47] Muhlenberg, "General Muhlenberg to General Gates, September 29, 1780," *The Life of Major-General Peter Muhlenberg of the Revolutionary Army*, 374

[48] Muhlenberg, "General Gates to General Muhlenberg, October 17, 1780, *The Life of Major-General Peter Muhlenberg of the Revolutionary Army*, 377

Chapter Five

The Present Moment is Critical

1780-1781

Determining Lieutenant Colonel Campbell's whereabouts and activities during the fall of 1780 is difficult. It appears he returned to Virginia in September (perhaps earlier) during which he possibly spoke to General Muhlenberg directly about the exchange of commands.[1] His time in Virginia was likely divided between visiting his family in Woodstock and supervising the recruitment efforts of his fellow officers in the 9th Virginia Regiment, to which he was still assigned until the proposed exchange with Lieutenant Colonel Taylor was finalized.[2]

General Baron von Steuben, who arrived in Richmond in late November to assume command of the continental forces in Virginia, provides a clue to Campbell's whereabouts in December in a letter to Governor Thomas Jefferson.

> *Lt. Col. Campbell of the 9th Va. Regiment, which is now at Fort Pitt, has orders to join his regiment but is unable to do so for want of $4,000 to pay the expenses of the journey.*[3]

---

[1] Muhlenberg, "General Muhlenberg to General Gates, September 29, 1780," *The Life of Major-General Peter Muhlenberg of the Revolutionary Army*, 374

[2] "Colonel Brodhead to General Steuben, January 17, 1780," *The Steuben Papers* (Microfilm).

[3] Julian P. Boyd, ed., "General Steuben to Governor Jefferson, December 16, 1780," *The Papers of Thomas Jefferson*, Vol. 4, (Princeton, NJ : Princeton University Press, 1951), 214

General Steuben requested that a warrant for $4,000 be made out to Campbell, "*so that the public service will not suffer by his longer detention in Richmond.*"[4]

A week later, Lieutenant Colonel Campbell, still in Richmond, presided over the court martial of a fellow officer.[5] He departed for Fort Pitt soon after and arrived on the frontier in mid-January with a message for Colonel Brodhead from General Steuben.[6] The precarious American situation in the South required greater assistance and resources, so the officers of the 9th Virginia Regiment who were in Virginia recruiting for replacements for their companies would not be returning to Fort Pitt with their new recruits.[7] Instead, they were to join a detachment being formed in Chesterfield County to march south to reinforce General Nathanael Greene's American southern army.

Lieutenant Colonel Campbell was also destined to march south, and he left Fort Pitt within days of delivering General Steuben's message. He arrived in Chesterfield County Courthouse in time to attend several meetings in mid-February of Virginian continental officers to finalize yet another new arrangement of the Virginia line. Supernumerary (surplus) officers without units to command formally resigned their commissions and six new regiments were formed.[8] Lieutenant Colonel Campbell was assigned to the 4th Regiment (formerly

---

[4] Boyd, ed., "General Steuben to Governor Jefferson, December 16, 1780," *The Papers of Thomas Jefferson*, Vol. 4 214

[5] "Court Martial Proceedings, December 23, 1780," *The Steuben Papers* (Microfilm).

[6] "Colonel Brodhead to General Steuben, January 17, 1780," *The Steuben Papers* (Microfilm).

[7] Ibid.

[8] William P. Palmer, ed., "Arrangement of the Virginia Line, 1781," *Calendar of Virginia State Papers*, Vol. 1, (Richmond, 1875), 410-413

the 11th Regiment) and with the colonel of that unit, John Neville, a captive of the British, Campbell became the ranking officer of the regiment.[9]

The new arrangement of the Virginia line was largely one on paper, however. In reality, two separate detachments of Virginian continentals (about 750 in total but very poorly outfitted and much reduced by illness) had already marched south to reinforce the American army under General Greene. These detachments were currently under the commands of Colonel John Green and Lieutenant Colonel Samuel Hawes, both of who were appointed to the reorganized 6th Virginia Regiment under the new arrangement.

General Steuben desired to send a third detachment of Virginia continentals to General Greene as soon as he could, but a severe shortage of clothing delayed their departure. The number of 18 month continentals reporting for duty was also less than expected. General Steuben informed General Greene in early February that Virginia would be at least 25% below its quota of continentals for 1781. This forced Steuben to reduce each regiment from 612 men to 412 men, (from nine companies to six companies per regiment) with one field officer, four captains, and fourteen subalterns (lieutenants and ensigns).[10]

It was at the last meeting of the Virginian continental officers on February 18th, that General Steuben selected the officers to lead the next detachment southward to reinforce

---

[9] Palmer, ed., "Arrangement of the Virginia Line, 1781," *Calendar of Virginia State Papers*, Vol. 1, 410-413

[10] Richard K. Showman, ed., "General Steuben to General Greene, February 3, 1781," *The Papers of General Nathanael Greene*, Vol. 7 (Chapel Hill, NC: The University of North Carolina Press, 1994), 250

General Greene.[11] As soon as the 400 men of the next detachment were finally supplied with proper clothing, Lieutenant Colonel Richard Campbell was to lead them south to reinforce General Greene.

General Nathanael Greene's American southern army was in desperate need of reinforcements in February 1781. Although General Daniel Morgan had scored a stunning American victory over the British at the Battle of Cowpens in mid-January 1781, he had also stirred General Charles Cornwallis to action. The British commander in the South, eager to undo the humiliation to British arms of the defeat at Cowpens, pursued General Greene's army into North Carolina.

General Greene realized the danger his army, inferior in both numbers and skill, was in and wisely retreated northward, crossing the Dan River in southern Virginia on February 15th. Everything now depended on Virginia, specifically the Virginia militia and continentals, to take the field and join General Greene. The American commander bluntly wrote to General Steuben that if Cornwallis pushed on across the river, his American army would be, *"ruined without reinforcements; but if exertions are made equal to the occasion all may yet have a favorable issue."*[12]

Greene's assertion was not tested; General Cornwallis made no attempt to cross the Dan River and instead, withdrew to Hillsborough, North Carolina. Relieved and encouraged (by reports of large militia reinforcements on the march to

---

[11] Showman, ed., "General Steuben to General Greene, February 3, 1781," *The Papers of General Nathanael Greene*, Vol. 7, 250

[12] Showman, ed., "General Greene to General Steuben, February 15, 1781," *The Papers of General Nathanael Greene*, Vol. 7, 292

him), General Greene re-crossed the Dan River and marched, cautiously, towards Hillsborough, hoping that several militia detachments that were reportedly on the march would catch up to him soon.

On February 25th, General Greene and his army, still waiting for the promised reinforcements, sat encamped twelve miles north of Hillsborough.[13] About 150 miles to the north, Lieutenant Colonel Campbell and 400 Virginia continentals finally set out from Chesterfield Courthouse to reinforce Greene's army.[14] Campbell's orders were to march the detachment 20 miles a day to Taylor's Ferry on the Roanoke River.[15] Once there, he would receive orders from General Greene directing the remainder of his march.

Lieutenant Colonel Campbell's men were unable to march as quickly as hoped, no doubt the result of poor footwear, and it took them over a week (instead of five days) to reach Taylor's Ferry.[16] Campbell wrote to General Greene to assure him that he would march by the, *"neareist and best route,"* to join Greene's army.[17]

One challenge, however, was that General Greene was on the move, reacting to General Cornwallis, who had moved his army westward. Greene and his troops were approximately 70 miles to the southwest of Campbell on the north bank of

---

[13] Showman, ed., "General Greene to General Steuben, February 25, 1781," *The Papers of General Nathanael Greene*, Vol. 7, 348
[14] Showman, ed., "General Steuben to General Greene, February 15, 1781," *The Papers of General Nathanael Greene*, Vol. 7, 362
[15] Ibid.
[16] Showman, ed., "Colonel Campbell to General Greene, March 3, 1781," *The Papers of General Nathanael Greene*, Vol. 7, 383
[17] Ibid.

Buffalo Creek.[18] An aide to General Greene responded to Campbell's dispatch from Taylor's Ferry on March 5th, stressing that Campbell should conduct forced marches to reach Greene as quickly as possible. *"The present moment is critical; therefore you will not lose an instant of time,"* wrote Greene's aide.[19]

Slowed by both bad shoes and a number of wagons carrying 600 stand of arms and the baggage of the detachment, Campbell's men took three days to march about 50 miles further south towards Hillsborough.[20] On March 8th, Lieutenant Colonel Campbell wrote to General Greene seeking orders. He informed Greene that he intended to march 17 miles (westward) and would so continue until he received orders.[21]

Major Ichabod Burnet, another aide to General Greene, replied to Campbell the next day from High Rock Ford on the Haw River, ordering him on behalf of General Greene to, *"proceed by forced marches on the most direct route to this place."*[22] Major Burnet added that Campbell's baggage should follow with a small guard.[23] Two more days passed before

---

[18] Showman, ed., "General Greene to General Caswell, March 3, 1781," *The Papers of General Nathanael Greene*, Vol. 7, 382

[19] Showman, ed., "Captain William Pierce Jr. to Colonel Richard Campbell, March 5, 1781," *The Papers of General Nathanael Greene*, Vol. 7, 394

[20] Showman, ed., "Lieutenant Colonel Campbell to General Greene, March 8, 1781," *The Papers of General Nathanael Greene*, Vol. 7, 411

[21] Ibid.

[22] Showman, ed., "Major Burnett to Lieutenant Colonel Campbell, March 9, 1781," *The Papers of General Nathanael Greene*, Vol. 7, 414

[23] Ibid.

Lieutenant Colonel Campbell finally caught up to General Greene's army.[24]

General Greene was undoubtedly relieved by Campbell's arrival, but the Virginia continentals were not the only troops to join Greene. General Richard Caswell of North Carolina arrived in camp with approximately 1,000 North Carolina militia and General Edward Stevens of Virginia also joined Greene's army with several hundred Virginia militia.[25] The situation had shifted dramatically in Greene's favor and he moved to exploit his advantage, marching his army westward towards Guilford Courthouse and the British army.[26]

While Campbell's continentals were incorporated into the Virginia brigade (which was commanded by General Isaac Huger of South Carolina) it is unclear whether they remained intact as a detachment or were divided among the other two Virginia detachments already under General Huger. Accounts of the Battle of Guilford Courthouse all focus on two Virginia regiments in the third line of General Greene's army, one commanded by Colonel John Green and the other commanded by Lieutenant Colonel Samuel Hawes. This left Lieutenant Colonel Campbell without a command, so according to most accounts of the battle, Campbell was attached to Colonel John Green's regiment.[27] Lieutenant Colonel Samuel Hawes, who

---

[24] Showman, ed., "General Greene to General Steuben, March 11, 1781," *The Papers of General Nathanael Greene*, Vol. 7, 427
[25] Lawrence E. Babits and Joshua B. Howard, *Long, Obstinate, and Bloody: The Battle of Guilford* Courthouse, (Chapel Hill, NC: The University of North Carolina Press, 2009), 48
[26] Showman, ed., "General Greene to Samuel Huntington, President of the Continental Congress, March 16, 1781," *The Papers of General Nathanael Greene*, Vol. 7, 433
[27] Babits and Howard, *Long, Obstinate, and Bloody: The Battle of Guilford Courthouse*, 73

outranked Campbell, assumed command of the detachment that Campbell had led southward.[28] However, comments about and changes made to the Virginia brigade by General Greene suggest that three distinct Virginia detachments existed in Greene's army at the time of the battle at Guilford Courthouse, and if this was so, it is likely that Lieutenant Colonel Campbell retained command of the troops he led to North Carolina and was attached to Colonel John Green's detachment for the battle.[29]

Battle of Guilford Courthouse

When General Greene and his army of over 4,000 men arrived at Guilford Courthouse on March 14th, he did so determined to attack the British as soon as possible.[30] Aware that Cornwallis and his roughly 2,000 man army of British veterans were just a few miles to the west, Greene posted strong reconnaissance parties several miles outside of Guilford Courthouse to prevent against surprise.[31]

---

[28] Babits and Howard, *Long, Obstinate, and Bloody: The Battle of Guilford Courthouse*, 74 and Showman, ed., "General Greene to Samuel Huntington, President of the Continental Congress, March 16, 1781," *The Papers of General Nathanael Greene*, Vol. 7, 433

[29] Dennis M. Conrad, ed., "General Greene to Colonel Davies, April 3, 1781," and "General Greene's Orders, April 4, 1781," and "General Greene to Major Burnett, April 5, 1781," *The Papers of General Nathanael Greene*, Vol. 8, (Chapel Hill, NC: The University of North Carolina Press, 1995), 43-44, 45, 55

[30] Babits and Howard, *Long, Obstinate, and Bloody: The Battle of Guilford Courthouse*, 77

[31] Babits and Howard, *Long, Obstinate, and Bloody: The Battle of Guilford Courthouse*, 219 and Showman, ed., "General Greene to Samuel Huntington, President of the Continental Congress, March 16, 1781," *The Papers of General Nathanael Greene*, Vol. 7, 433

General Greene's caution was warranted, for as soon as General Cornwallis learned of the American presence at Guilford Courthouse, Cornwallis moved to strike.[32] The British were on the march before dawn and their advance guard, led by Lieutenant Colonel Banastre Tarleton, clashed with the American reconnaissance party commanded by Lieutenant Colonel "Light Horse" Harry Lee. The skirmish near the New Garden Meeting House, was reported to General Greene, who prepared the main American army for battle. He described his arrangement to Congress the day after the battle.

> *The Army was drawn up in three lines. The front line was composed of the North Carolina Militia...the second line of Virginia Militia...the third line consisting of two Brigades, one of Virginia and one of Maryland continental Troops....*[33]

Greene was following General Morgan's example of a defense in depth. He supported his first line of militia with some of his best troops and his cavalry posted upon each flank.

General Greene's strategy, like Morgan's before him, was simple. The militia troops of the first and second line were not expected to stop the enemy, just wear them down. If they put up the fight that Greene hoped, his third line of Virginia, Maryland and Delaware continentals, rested and ready to

---

[32] Babits and Howard, *Long, Obstinate, and Bloody: The Battle of Guilford Courthouse*, 50
[33] Showman, ed., "General Greene to Samuel Huntington, President of the Continental Congress, March 16, 1781," *The Papers of General Nathanael Greene*, Vol. 7, 434

fight, should be able to win the day against the worn down enemy.

The Great Salisbury Road passed through the middle of Greene's first and second lines and was the route that General Cornwallis and his army followed in their attack. Both armies were bisected by this road until it reached Greene's third line. At the third line, most of the American continentals were posted to the north side of the road and the American left flank bended rearward to parallel the road and protect the flank.

The order of placement at Greene's third line from the road northward (to the right) was the 2nd Maryland Regiment, then the 1st Maryland Regiment, then Lt. Colonel Samuel Hawes's Virginia detachment followed by Colonel John Green's Virginia detachment (of which Lieutenant Colonel Campbell was with).[34] The two Virginia detachments were brigaded under General Isaac Huger while the two Maryland regiments, bolstered by a detachment of Delaware continentals, were brigaded under Colonel Otho Holland Williams of Maryland. Each of General Greene's four continental units comprised around 400 men, so his continentals actually numbered less than General Cornwallis's army, but Greene hoped that the action at the first and second line would significantly reduce British numbers and organization, allowing his rested continentals to stand and defeat the remnants of the enemy.[35]

Greene's third line sat more than 500 yards behind his second line, more than he would have desired, but the terrain between the two lines did not allow for the continentals to be posted any closer. Lieutenant Colonel Campbell and his

---

[34] Babits and Howard, *Long, Obstinate, and Bloody: The Battle of Guilford Courthouse*, 69-74
[35] Ibid., 220

fellow continentals waited for the enemy upon rising, wooded ground. To the front of most of the continentals on the third line was a vale that had been cleared for farming, but the clearing did not extend all the way across the front of Campbell's position on the right flank. He could see the open vale to his left, but for many of the Virginians with Colonel Green and Lieutenant Colonel Campbell on the right flank of the American 3rd line, a wooded, sloping landscape faced them.[36]

General Cornwallis began his advance upon General Greene's main army around noon. Lieutenant Colonel Campbell undoubtedly heard the 20 minute artillery duel between the two sides that preceded the British advance.[37] Once the cannon stopped, there was likely several minutes of silence as the British army maneuvered past their cannon and advanced towards Greene's first line. A loud volley of small arms fire followed by scattered musket and rifle fire from the 1,000 or so militia at the first line would have broken the silence. This signaled the disappointing resistance of the American first line, most of who, if they fired at all, only fired one shot before they broke and ran to the rear.[38] Another pause occurred while the British pushed forward to the second line, 300 yards beyond the first line.

---

[36] Banastre Tarleton, "Battle of Guilford Map," *A History of the Campaigns of 1780-1781 in the Southern Provinces of North America*, (NH: AYER Company, 1999), 277
    Originally printed in 1787
[37] Showman, ed., "General Greene to Samuel Huntington, President of the Continental Congress, March 16, 1781," *The Papers of General Nathanael Greene*, Vol. 7, 434
[38] Ibid.

It was at this point, some 500 yards to his front and out of view, that Lieutenant Colonel Campbell would have noticed a surge of gunfire and combat. Many of the Virginia militiamen at the second line stood firm and a pitched fight over broken, wooded, terrain ensued. The sound of battle, specifically gunfire and the shouts of commands and distress, must have been both intense and unnerving to Campbell and his men.

Finally, about ninety minutes after the first cannon shots kicked off the attack, the enemy appeared before the continentals from the woods across the cleared vale to their front.[39] The first to arrive was the British 33rd Regiment, led by Lieutenant Colonel James Webster, joined by some light infantry and jagers. They were tired, somewhat disordered by the heavy fighting through the American second line, and significantly outnumbered by General Greene's continentals, yet Webster ordered his men forward down the steep slope and into the vale. They were pummeled by musket and cannon fire and quickly retreated back up the far slope.[40]

The battle now shifted to the opposite side of the American line where the Maryland troops were posted. Brigadier-General Charles O' Hara, wounded earlier in the advance, led 600 British Guards against the 2nd Maryland Regiment, who shockingly broke and ran in the face of the attack, abandoning two of General Greene's four cannon at the third line.[41] The 1st Maryland Regiment, whose left flank and rear were now exposed and threatened, faced about and engaged the British Guards. The struggle became severe and in many cases hand

---

[39] Babits and Howard, *Long, Obstinate, and Bloody: The Battle of Guilford Courthouse*, 142
[40] Ibid., 145
[41] Ibid., 147

to hand. The arrival of Lieutenant Colonel William Washington's American cavalry momentarily swung the struggle in the Americans' favor. British cannon fire, however, which hit friend and foe alike, broke up the American attack and the two sides disengaged.[42]

Lieutenant Colonel Campbell, with Colonel Green's regiment on the other side of the American line, did not participate in the pivotal fighting on the left flank of the American line. In fact, they had engaged in relatively little fighting up to that point. As a result, Colonel Green's Virginians were the best choice to cover the American retreat from Guilford Courthouse when General Greene gave the order to do so following the flight of the 2nd Maryland Regiment.[43] The British made a half-hearted attempt to pursue Greene's army, but most of Cornwallis's force was exhausted, so the fighting between the few troops that pursued and Colonel Green's Virginians was limited, and the enemy pursuit easily checked.[44]

The Battle of Guilford Courthouse was a British victory, but it came at a high price. Approximately a quarter of General Cornwallis's troops were casualties and although many would eventually rejoin the army, his force was exhausted, weak and in dire need of re-supply and rest.[45] Cornwallis remained at Guilford Courthouse for several days to tend to the wounded and then marched south, towards Cross

---

[42] Ibid., 162
[43] Showman, ed., "General Greene to Samuel Huntington, President of the Continental Congress, March 16, 1781," *The Papers of General Nathanael Greene*, Vol. 7, 435
[44] Ibid.
[45] Babits and Howard, *Long, Obstinate, and Bloody: The Battle of Guilford Courthouse*, 173

Creek and eventually Wilmington, where he was able to obtain desperately needed supplies from the British navy.

He remained in Wilmington for several weeks and then surprised General Greene by marching north in late April to Virginia, where several large British detachments were operating. Cornwallis hoped his movement north would cause General Greene to pursue him and relieve the British garrisons in South Carolina.[46]

Ironically, General Greene had initially followed Cornwallis southward after Guilford Courthouse, determined to attack despite the departure of most of his militia after the battle.[47] Supply problems prevented Greene from catching Cornwallis and once the opportunity to attack had passed, General Greene decided to adjust his focus and, *"Carry the War immediately into South Carolina."*[48] He reasoned to General Washington that, *"The Enemy will be obliged to follow us or give up their posts in that State."* [49]

As it turned out, neither commander reacted the way the other expected. Cornwallis remained in Wilmington for most of April while Greene marched south to strike British posts in South Carolina. On the day that General Greene engaged British troops on the outskirts of Camden, South Carolina, General Cornwallis commenced his march north to Virginia, hoping, unsuccessfully, that such a movement would draw General Greene northward.

---

[46] Tarleton, "General Cornwallis to General Phillips, April 24th, 1781," 328-329

[47] Showman, ed., "General Greene to Colonel Lee, March 22, 1781," *The Papers of General Nathanael Greene*, Vol. 7, 461

[48] Showman, ed., "General Greene to General Washington, March 29, 1781," *The Papers of General Nathanael Greene*, Vol. 7, 481

[49] Ibid.

General Greene Marches South

Prior to his march to South Carolina (in early April) General Greene adjusted the command structure and organization of his Virginia continentals. Colonel John Green, suffering from rheumatism, was granted leave to return to Virginia to recover his health.[50] He carried with him an appeal from the Virginia officers with General Greene that the separate detachments of Virginia continentals assigned to Greene's army be organized into formal regiments. Lieutenant Colonel Campbell and his fellow officers noted that they,

> *Observe the disadvantages of their current situation – in detachments & not Regimented. These include inattention of the officers to the soldiers, a desire to Retire from Camp, and a decline in discipline and subordination. Detached commands are temporary & uncertain, & the duty of the officers unequal and unjust; when the regiments are formed, the absent officers will be more accountable to their commanders.*[51]

General Greene, aware of the discipline and morale issues among the Virginia officers, endorsed their appeal and wrote his own letter to Colonel William Davies at Chesterfield County Courthouse.

---

[50] Conrad, ed., "General Greene to General Steuben, April 4, 1781," *The Papers of General Nathanael Greene*, Vol. 8, 50
[51] Conrad, ed., "Virginia Officers Serving with the Southern Army, April 3, 1781," *The Papers of General Nathanael Greene*, Vol. 8, 43

The disagreeable situation of the detachments serving with this army from the State of Virginia, and the complaints of all ranks of officers from their not being Regimented induces me to wish that the first and second Regiment should be immediately formed, and the Officers sent forward without loss of time. While the troops act by detachment and the officers uncertain whether they will command the same men, they will not pay that attention to the discipline of the troops which the good of the service requires.[52]

With the departure of Colonel Green and the uncertainty of action from Virginia, General Greene decided to reorganize the Virginia continentals himself, ordering that two regiments, with, *"great equality,"* be formed from among the three detachments.[53] Lieutenant Colonel Richard Campbell assumed command of the 1st Virginia Regiment and Lieutenant Colonel Samuel Hawes commanded the 2nd Virginia.[54] Brigadier-General Isaac Huger continued to command the brigaded Virginia continentals, which numbered just over 500 officers and men, split between the two regiments.[55]

---

[52] Conrad, ed., "General Greene to Colonel Davies, April 3, 1781," *The Papers of General Nathanael Greene*, Vol. 8, 43-44
[53] Conrad, ed., "General Greene's Orders, April 4, 1781," *The Papers of General Nathanael Greene*, Vol. 8, 45
[54] Conrad, ed., "General Greene to Major Burnett, April 5, 1781," *The Papers of General Nathanael Greene*, Vol. 8, 55
[55] National Archives, "Field Return of Infantry serving in the Southern Army of the United States Commanded by the Honorable Major-General Greene accounting for the killed etc. in the action of the 25th Instant," *Papers of the Continental Congress*, Vol. 2, 167

One of the ensigns in Campbell's 1st Virginia was his eldest son, Archibald.[56] Ensign Campbell likely marched south with his father in February, but who he served with at Guilford Courthouse is uncertain.

Colonel Green was not the only Virginia officer who returned to Virginia in early April. Captain Thomas Edmonds also returned home and carried with him a letter to Governor Thomas Jefferson penned by Lieutenant Colonel Campbell. It was essentially a plea for assistance for the troops that Campbell had led south six weeks earlier.

I am under the necessity from my own feelings to inform your Exelency of the destressed situation of the Soldiers in my Regiment for want of Cloathing. When I marched from the State of Virga. to join the Army I received a Pare of Overalls for Each Soldier, made of Ozenbrigs which did not last them more than two or three Weeks, and also a shirt for Each Soldier which are intirely worn out and them distressed for every kind of Cloathing Except Coats. I have obtained leave of Genl. Greene to send an officer to the state of Virginia, in order to procure such Cloathing as the men stand most in kneed of and Capt. Edmonds is the officer appointed for that business, who will hand you this, And I hope your Excellency will take the matter under your consideration, and send out such Cloathing as Capt. Edmonds will inform you is most wanting. As for the news of the Armey I Refer to the Barer Capt. Edmonds.[57]

---

[56] "April 5, 1781," *Orderly Book of Nathanael Greene, April 1 – July 25, 1781*, (Huntington Library)

[57] Julian P. Boyd., ed., Lieutenant Colonel Richard Campbell to Governor Thomas Jefferson, April 3, 1781," *The Papers of Thomas Jefferson*, Vol. 5, (Princeton, NJ: Princeton University Press, 1952), 325

Despite the condition of his Virginia continentals, General Greene commenced his march to South Carolina on April 6th, marching from Ramsey's Mill in central North Carolina on a southwesterly route. His destination was Camden, South Carolina, where the British maintained a key outpost to control the central part of South Carolina. A week into the march, General Greene lamented to Governor Abner Nash of North Carolina that the severe shortage of horses threatened the ability of the army to move and gather enough provision to subsist on.

> *The means of transportation is a distressing circumstance, and unless every aid is given, I fear it will soon be out of our power, either to move or subsist our army in a fixed Camp.*[58]

Although transport woes slowed his march, it did not stop Greene's army, and they encamped just a few miles north of Camden on April 19th. General Greene was disappointed to discover that the enemy garrison under Lord Francis Rawdon was larger than he expected, and the fortifications, much stronger.[59] Rawdon had over 1,000 troops at Camden, and although most were actually American provincials and loyalist militia fighting for the King, the fortifications that protected Camden were strong.[60]

---

[58] Conrad, ed., "General Greene to Governor Abner Nash, April 13, 1781," *The Papers of General Nathanael Greene*, Vol. 8, 89

[59] Conrad, ed., "General Greene to Samuel Huntington, President of the Continental Congress, April 22, 1781," *The Papers of General Nathanael Greene*, Vol. 8, 129-131

[60] Patrick O'Kelly, *Nothing but Blood and Slaughter: The Revolutionary War in the Carolinas,* Vol. 3, (Blue House Tavern Press, 2005), 202, 205

General Greene, with approximately 1,250 troops and several cannon, opted not to attack Camden, but instead, draw the enemy out to fight.[61] He placed his army upon Hobkirk's Hill, just two miles north of Camden, and waited. They were encamped in the same order they were to fight. Lieutenant Colonel Campbell's regiment of Virginians held the right flank of the American line. To their left was Lieutenant Colonel Hawes's Virginians. The road to Camden passed to the left of Hawes, and on the other side was the 1st Maryland Regiment commanded by Lieutenant Colonel John Gumby. To their left was the 2nd Maryland Regiment under Lieutenant Colonel Benjamin Ford.[62] Altogether General Greene's continentals surpassed 1,250 officers and men.[63]

Three six pound cannon arrived on April 25th, and were placed in the road between the Virginia and Maryland continentals. Approximately 250 North Carolina militia along with Lieutenant Colonel William Washington's continental cavalry were placed in reserve behind the continentals.[64] General Greene had strong pickets in the woods to the front of Hobkirk Hill and Captain Robert Kirkwood's company of Delaware continentals were posted in the woods between the

---

[61] National Archives, "Field Return of Infantry serving in the Southern Army of the United States Commanded by the Honorable Major-General Greene accounting for the killed etc. in the action of the 25th Instant," *Papers of the Continental Congress*, Vol. 2, 167

[62] Conrad, ed., "General Greene to Samuel Huntington, President of the Continental Congress, April 27, 1781," *The Papers of General Nathanael Greene*, Vol. 8, 155-156

[63] National Archives, "Field Return of Infantry serving in the Southern Army of the United States Commanded by the Honorable Major-General Greene accounting for the killed etc. in the action of the 25th Instant," *Papers of the Continental Congress*, Vol. 2, 167

[64] Robert E. Lee, ed., *The Revolutionary War Memoirs of General Henry Lee*, (New York: Da Capo, 1998), 335

pickets and main defensive line to support the pickets if they were attacked.[65]

Battle of Hobkirk's Hill

On the morning of April 25th Lord Rawdon led a force of over 900 troops, including armed, *"Musicians...Drummers & in short everyone that could carry a Firelock,"* against General Greene's army on Hobkirk's Hill.[66] Rawdon was concerned about reports of American reinforcements marching to join Greene. He hoped his sudden strike at Greene would destroy and scatter the American army much like General Cornwallis's attack on General Gates at Camden eight months earlier had.

Surprise was crucial to Rawdon's success, so he led his outnumbered men on a circuitous route through thick woods to hit the American left flank. Many of Greene's continentals were away from the line, washing their clothing in a stream behind Hobkirk's Hill.[67] Fortunately for the Americans, General Greene's pickets discovered Rawdon's approached and gave the alarm.[68]

General Greene's account of the battle provides a good picture of what occurred. He informed Congress that,

---

[65] Conrad, ed., "General Greene to Samuel Huntington, President of the Continental Congress, April 22, 1781," *The Papers of General Nathanael Greene*, Vol. 8, 155

[66] Conrad, ed., "Lord Rawdon to General Cornwallis, April 25-26, 1781, Note 1," *The Papers of General Nathanael Greene*, Vol. 8, 157

[67] Lee, 336

[68] Conrad, ed., "General Greene to Samuel Huntington, President of the Continental Congress, April 22, 1781," *The Papers of General Nathanael Greene*, Vol. 8, 155

> *About 11 oClock on the Morning of the 25th [of April] our advanced Piquets were fired upon, who gave the Enemy a warm reception. The line was formed in an instant, General Huger's Brigade [of Virginians] upon the right of the road, Col. [Otho] Williams's Brigade of Marylanders on the left....*[69]

General Greene reported that his pickets fought well, giving the troops posted on Hobkirk Hill time to prepare. Greene explained to Congress that

> *As the Enemy were found to be advancing only with a small front, Lieut Col. Ford with the 2nd Maryland Regiment had orders to advance and flank them upon the left, Lieut Col. Campbell had orders to do the like upon the right. Col. Gunby with the first Maryland Regiment and Lieut Col. Haws with the second Virginia Regiment, had orders to advance down the Hill and charge them in front.*[70]

General Greene had ordered a double envelopment of the enemy, a maneuver long prized by commanders throughout history. Alas, Lord Rawdon noted the threat to his flanks and ordered his reserve forward to extend his own front and protect them. General Greene reported that,

---

[69] Conrad, ed., "General Greene to Samuel Huntington, President of the Continental Congress, April 22, 1781," *The Papers of General Nathanael Greene*, Vol. 8, 155

[70] Ibid.

The whole line was soon engaged in close firing, and the Artillery under Col. Harrison playing on their front. The Enemy were staggered in all quarters, and upon the left were retiring while our troops continued to advance.[71]

Unfortunately for the Americans, two companies on the right flank of the 1st Maryland became disordered in the fighting and Colonel Gunby ordered the rest of the regiment to halt and reform on the two disordered companies. General Greene explained the impact of this retrograde movement upon his army.

This impressed the whole Regiment with an Idea of a retreat, and communicated itself to the 2d Regiment which immediately followed the first on their retiring. Both were rallied but it was too late, the Enemy had gained the Hill and obliged the Artillery to retire.[72]

Over on the far right of the American line, Lieutenant Colonel Campbell's regiment had also, *"got into some disorder and fallen back a little."*[73] Campbell rallied his men and at some point was wounded with, *"a slight contusion on his thigh,"* but he and his men remained in the fight.[74]

---

[71] Conrad, ed., "General Greene to Samuel Huntington, President of the Continental Congress, April 22, 1781," *The Papers of General Nathanael Greene,* Vol. 8, 156

[72] Ibid.

[73] Ibid., 157

[74] Conrad, ed., "General Greene to Colonel Henry Lee, Jr., April 28, 1781," *The Papers of General Nathanael Greene,* Vol. 8, 169, and National Archives, "List of Commissioned Officers Killed, Wounded and Captured in the action before Camden, 25 April, 1781," *Papers of the Continental Congress,* Vol. 2, Roll # 175, 168a

With three of his four regiments, as well as his cannon, forced back, however, General Greene, who was with Lieutenant Colonel Hawes's regiment near the road at the bottom of Hobkirk's Hill, was obliged to order Hawes to retire as well.[75]

The American army retreated several miles north and encamped. Despite the setback, General Greene reported to Congress that the army was not, *"materially different."*[76] In fact, although Lord Rawdon emerged victorious by forcing Greene to retreat, each side lost approximately the same amount of men, about 270 each, so little had effectively changed.[77] Lieutenant Colonel Campbell's regiment suffered 33 casualties in the battle, about a third of the number lost in Lieutenant Colonel Hawes's regiment.[78]

General Greene remained with his army near Camden for several days hoping to strike at the diminished British garrison. In a letter to the Chevalier de La Luzerne, a French ally and friend, Greene doggedly proclaimed what became his mantra in the south.

We fight, get beat, rise and fight again. The whole Country is one continued scene of blood and slaughter.[79]

---

[75] Conrad, ed., "General Greene to Samuel Huntington, President of the Continental Congress, April 22, 1781," *The Papers of General Nathanael Greene*, Vol. 8, 157

[76] Ibid.

[77] O'Kelley, 199, 202

[78] National Archives, "Field Return of Infantry serving in the Southern Army of the United States Commanded by the Honorable Major-General Greene accounting for the killed etc. in the action of the 25th Instant," *Papers of the Continental Congress*, Vol. 2, 167

[79] Conrad, ed., "General Greene to the Chevalier de La Luzerne,, April 28, 1781," *The Papers of General Nathanael Greene*, Vol. 8, 168

British Outposts in South Carolina

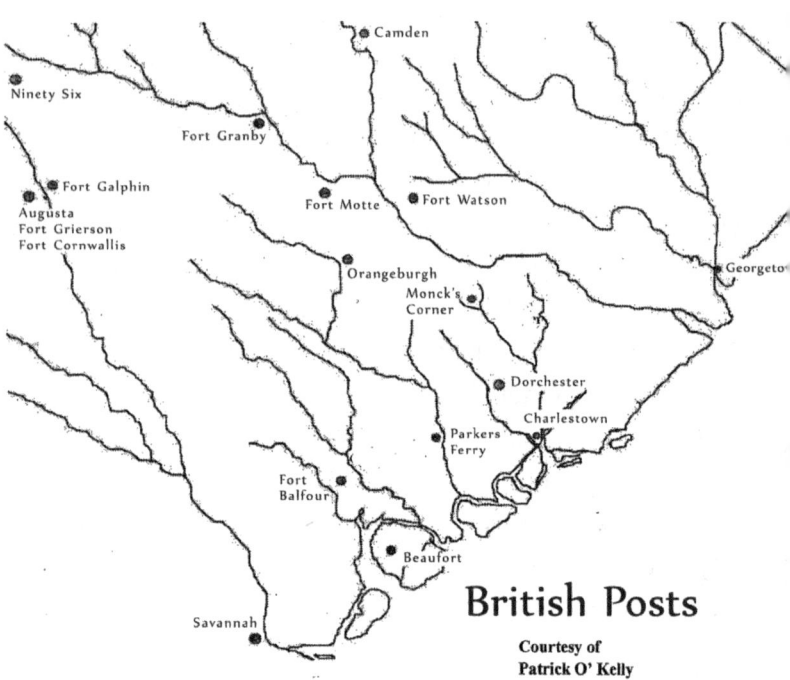

Chapter Six

He was the Great Soldier and the Firm Patriot.

1781

On the same day General Greene described his struggles to the Chevalier de La Luzerne, Greene marched his army a few miles further north to Rugley's Mill, about thirteen miles from Camden, *"for the sake of recruiting our Cattle"*.[1] Greene complained to Congress that the promised reinforcement of 2,000 Virginia militia had yet to arrive and that many of his Maryland continentals were leaving the army because their terms of enlistment had expired.[2] *"Maryland has neglected us altogether,"* wrote Greene, *"not a Man has joined us from that State since I have been in the Department."*[3] General Greene went on to despair of his supply situation.

> *I can see no place where an Army of any considerable force can subsist for any length of time: and the horses are so destroyed in this Country that subsistence cannot be drawn from a distance. The Country is so laid to waste and the means of transportation so unequal to the business of collecting supplies from a distance for an Army, that*

---

[1] Conrad, ed., "General Greene to Samuel Huntington, President of the Continental Congress, May 5, 1781,"*The Papers of General Nathanael Greene*, Vol. 8, 206
[2] Ibid.
[3] Ibid.

> *it is difficult for me to conceive how an Army is to be subsisted in this Country....*[4]

In addition to his concern about provisions for his army, General Greene was also aware that General Cornwallis had finally marched from Wilmington, North Carolina with his rested army.[5] Greene was initially uncertain of Cornwallis's destination and presumed he would head for South Carolina to assist Lord Rawdon. The American commander soon concluded, however, that Cornwallis was marching to Virginia, instead. Relieved as he was to not have 1,500 British troops coming after him, the arrival in Camden of 500 Tories under Colonel John Watson on May 7th, forced General Greene to move his army further north, away from Camden.[6] This proved fortuitous because Lord Rawdon marched out from Camden the next day with his reinforced army to give battle. General Greene described what happened to Colonel Henry Lee.

> *Lord Rawdon came out yesterday morning as I expected he would, and I suppose, with an expectation of finding us at the old encampment. I did not like our new position to risk an action in, and ordered the troops to take a new position at this place, four miles still higher up the river.... The enemy came up in front of our encampment, and*

---

[4] Conrad, ed., "General Greene to Samuel Huntington, President of the Continental Congress, May 5, 1781,"*The Papers of General Nathanael Greene*, Vol. 8, 206-207

[5] Conrad, ed., "General Greene to General Francis Marion, May 6, 1781,"*The Papers of General Nathanael Greene*, Vol. 8, 211

[6] Conrad, ed., "Note 3," *The Papers of General Nathanael Greene*, Vol. 8, 229

drew up in order of battle, but did not dare to attempt to cross the creek; and after waiting an hour or two, retired suddenly towards Camden.[7]

Rawdon's attempted attack upon Greene was apparently a last swipe at his adversary before he evacuated and burned Camden and marched back to Charleston. Late on the evening of May 10th, just two days after Rawdon's advance on Greene, the American general learned of Rawdon's departure.[8] General Greene viewed Rawdon's withdrawal from Camden as the beginning of a general British abandonment of the South Carolina interior and he quickly moved to exploit this development. Greene ordered the several detachments that had been operating separately in the state under General Thomas Sumter, General Francis Marion, and Lieutenant Colonel Henry Lee, to strike British posts along the Congaree River before their garrisons escaped.[9] General Sumter captured the British garrison at Orangeburg with his detachment of South Carolina militia and General Francis Marion and Lieutenant Colonel Henry Lee captured Fort Motte with their detachments.[10]

Lieutenant Colonel Campbell and the rest of Greene's main army followed in the wake of the victories of Lee, Marion, and Sumter. With British control of the South Carolina countryside

---

[7] Conrad, ed., "General Greene to Colonel Henry Lee, Jr., May 9, 1781,"*The Papers of General Nathanael Greene*, Vol. 8, 227-228

[8] Conrad, ed., "Captain Nathaniel Pendleton to General Thomas Sumter, May 10, 1781,"*The Papers of General Nathanael Greene*, Vol. 8, 236

[9] Conrad, ed., "General Greene to Samuel Huntington, President of the Continental Congress, May 14, 1781,"*The Papers of General Nathanael Greene*, Vol. 8, 250-251

[10] Ibid.

crumbling, General Greene turned his attention to the last significant British outpost in the interior of the state, Ninety-Six.

Siege of Ninety-Six

Ever since his march into South Carolina in April, General Greene viewed the British outpost at Ninety-Six in the western part of the state as a key objective to regain control of South Carolina's interior. He informed Congress in mid-May that

> *When we began our march towards Camden from Deep River* [North Carolina] *I wrote to General* [Andrew] *Pickens to endeavor to collect a body of Militia to lay siege to Augusta and Ninety-Six, and both places are now invested....*[11]

It was now time for Greene to march his main army westward to besiege and capture these outposts. While General Greene focused on Ninety-Six, he ordered Lieutenant-Colonel Lee and his legion of cavalry and infantry, who had already helped capture Fort Watson, Fort Motte, and Fort Granby, to march westward and join General Pickens at Augusta, Georgia to reduce the British outposts there.[12]

Greene and his army reached the outskirts of Ninety-Six on May 22st. He commented to Lieutenant-Colonel Lee that he found the post, *"much better fortified and garrison much*

---

[11] Conrad, ed., "General Greene to Samuel Huntington, President of the Continental Congress, May 14, 1781,"*The Papers of General Nathanael Greene*, Vol. 8, 250-251

[12] Conrad, ed., "General Greene to Colonel Henry Lee, Jr., May 16, 1781,"*The Papers of General Nathanael Greene*, Vol. 8, 272

stronger in regular troops than was expected."[13] This was not completely accurate, for the troops General Greene believed were British regulars were actually American provincials from New York and New Jersey, outfitted in redcoats.

The entire garrison at Ninety-Six numbered approximately 1,250 men, all American loyalists under the command of Lieutenant-Colonel John Cruger, a prominent New York loyalist and experienced provincial officer.[14] Protecting Cruger and his men were a series of fortifications beginning with a sturdy palisade wall of upright logs that surrounded the one hundred square yard village of Ninety-Six.[15] Several of the buildings in the village served as fortified block houses and a high mound of dirt and thick layer of abatis encircled the village.[16] Just outside the western wall of the village stood a three story brick jail, another strongpoint. It overlooked a ravine through which the water supply of the village flowed. A trench was dug from the jail to the bottom of the ravine to allow the garrison to retrieve water under cover.

The village and jail were the interior defenses of Lieutenant-Colonel Cruger's fortified position. Two additional fortified posts protected the village from direct assault.

To the west of Ninety-Six, on the opposite side of the ravine, was a stockade fort that guarded the western approach to the village. It consisted of a wooden palisade wall connected to several block houses. An earthen parapet, deep

---

[13] Conrad, ed., "General Greene to Colonel Henry Lee, Jr., May 22, 1781,"*The Papers of General Nathanael Greene*, Vol. 8, 291-292
[14] Robert M. Dunkerly and Eric K. Williams, *Old Ninety-Six: A History and Guide*, (Charleston, SC: A History Press, 2006), 66
[15] Ibid. 43
[16] Ibid., 44

ditch and abatis, were also placed in front of the palisade wall as additional obstacles. Another trench linked this position with the village.[17]

One hundred yards northwest of the village was Cruger's strongest position, an eight point star redoubt with three 3 pound cannon that defended the northern and eastern approach to Ninety-Six. A steep fourteen foot high earthen wall, deep ditch and thick abatis made Lieutenant Colonel Cruger's star redoubt a formidable position and the key to the defense of Ninety-Six.[18]

On his first evening at Ninety-Six, General Greene ordered the construction of an artillery battery just seventy yards from the star redoubt.[19] Not only was this a breach of siege warfare etiquette, which called for the besieging army to summon the besieged to surrender before actually commencing a siege, but it was also foolishly too close to the enemy and Lieutenant-Colonel Cruger exploited Greene's mistake. The following evening, while a detachment of General Greene's troops and a number of slaves worked on the artillery battery under cover of darkness, a sortie from Cruger's redoubt suddenly struck. Several of Greene's men were killed in the raid and the rest fled to the rear, abandoning their entrenching tools, which Cruger's men happily retrieved.[20]

After several days, General Greene, under the guidance of his chief engineer, Colonel Thaddeus Kosciuszko of Poland, began a more traditional siege, opening his first parallel (trench) much further back from the enemy on May 28th.[21]

---

[17] Dunkerly and Williams, *Old Ninety-Six: A History and Guide*, 48-49, 51
[18] Ibid., 40-41
[19] Ibid., 31
[20] Dunkerly and Williams, *Old Ninety-Six: A History and Guide*, 31
[21] Ibid.

The greater distance limited the effectiveness of enemy fire from the redoubt (and vice versa once the American battery opened up) and allowed the Americans to complete their first parallel by June 1st.[22]

The absence from camp of General Isaac Huger, who returned to his home to address personal matters, and the illness of Lieutenant Colonel Hawes, left Lieutenant Colonel Campbell as the ranking officer among the Virginia continentals.[23] Major Smith Snead assisted Campbell with command of the 1st Virginia, replacing Major Thomas Ridley, who had been designated a supernumerary officer in the new arrangement of the Virginia line adopted in February, but had remained with Greene's army, essentially as a volunteer.[24]

The completion of the first parallel was immediately followed by the construction of several zig-zag trenches (called saps) that extended from the first parallel towards the enemy. These were used to protect Greene's troops as they slowly advanced forward towards the redoubt to ultimately construct a second parallel, closer to the star redoubt.

Life in the trenches was hard and grew more dangerous the closer the saps advanced to the redoubt. General Greene rotated his troops back and forth from the trenches to camp (which was nearly a mile in the rear) to allow adequate rest from the hard labor under the scorching summer sun.[25] The South Carolina clay was difficult to move, made especially so

---

[22] Ibid.
[23] Conrad, ed., "General Huger to General Greene, May 27, 1781," and "General Greene to Major Thomas Hill, May 30, 1781,"*The Papers of General Nathanael Greene*, Vol. 8, 316, 330
[24] "May 28, 1781," *Orderly Book of Nathanael Greene, April 1 – July 25, 1781*, (Huntington Library).
[25] Dunkerly and Williams, *Old Ninety-Six: A History and Guide*, 31

by constant enemy fire. While work parties struggled to advance the saps and construct the second parallel, they were guarded by detachments of troops who kept a lookout for new enemy sorties.

Back in camp, other troops constructed the implements of a siege, specifically gabions (large woven baskets to be filled with dirt that formed the foundation of the earthworks that protected the trenches) and fascines (large bundles of sticks used to support the trench walls. They also tended to routine camp duty, wood, water, weapons maintenance, etc. and rested whenever they were able.

General Greene also rotated the supervision of the trenches among his officers and chief engineer, Colonel Kosciuszko. Lieutenant Colonel Campbell served as officer of the day on May 29th, during the construction of the first parallel, and again six days later on June 4th the day after the second parallel was completed.[26] With his lines now only sixty yards from Cruger's star redoubt, General Greene instructed Colonel Otho Williams of Maryland to send a summons to Cruger to surrender.[27] Cruger declined to surrender and launched several night raids on the second parallel and the saps extending from it in an effort to disrupt Greene's progress.[28] The evening sorties and steady fire from the redoubt, as well as the mounting fatigue of Greene's troops, did indeed slow his progress, and he expressed his frustration to Congress on June 9th.

---

[26] "May 28, and June 3, 1781," *Orderly Book of Nathanael Greene, April 1 – July 25, 1781*, (Huntington Library).
[27] Conrad, ed., "Colonel Otho Williams to Colonel John Cruger, June 3, 1781," *The Papers of General Nathanael Greene*, Vol. 8, 339
[28] Dunkerly and Williams, *Old Ninety-Six: A History and Guide*, 33

> *We have been prosecuting the Siege at this place with all possible diligence with our little force, but for want of more assistance the approaches have gone on exceeding slow, and our poor Fellows are worne out with fatigue, being constantly on duty every other Day and sometimes every Day. The works are strong and extensive. The position difficult to approach and the Ground extremely hard. The Garrison numerous and formidable when compared with our little force. They have sallied more or less every Night; but have been constantly driven in.*[29]

General Greene added the observation that British reinforcements had reportedly arrived in Charleston and that he expected a force would soon be sent from there to Ninety Six to relieve the garrison.[30]

The day following Greene's letter, the Americans completed their third parallel, just yards from the abatis and ditch in front of the star redoubt and two days after that, they constructed a thirty foot high wooden tower at the third parallel to allow parties of riflemen to fire over the fourteen foot high walls of the redoubt.[31]

The defenders in the redoubt responded by raising the walls higher with sand bags and firing red-hot cannonballs at the tower.[32] The first measure was somewhat effective but the

---

[29] Conrad, ed., "General Greene to Samuel Huntington, President of the Continental Congress, June 9, 1781,"*The Papers of General Nathanael Greene*, Vol. 8, 363-364
[30] Ibid.
[31] Dunkerly and Williams, *Old Ninety-Six: A History and Guide*, 35-36
[32] Ibid., 36

second failed completely and the riflemen kept up their deadly fire.

A few days prior to the construction of the tower, Colonel Kosciuszko had commenced the construction of a tunnel at the third parallel that he hoped would extend to the wall of the redoubt.[33] He intended to blow up a section of the redoubt to allow the Americans to storm through, but the rock hard clay made slowed progress on the mine and it was never completed.[34]

Although most of General Greene's attention and effort was focused on the star redoubt, he did authorize an attempt to burn the town of Ninety-Six with flaming arrows shot from the muskets of some of his troops.[35] The effort failed, but must have been a spectacle to witness.

In mid-June numerous reports reached General Greene of a large British force, some 2,000 men strong, that was marching to Ninety Six to lift the siege. Greene hoped that detachments under General Sumter and General Pickens could at least slow this force enough to allow his men to successfully complete the siege, but they were unsuccessful.

Realizing that time had run out to see the siege through, General Greene resorted to one last desperate measure. He ordered that the star redoubt and the stockade to the west of Ninety Six, be stormed on June 18th. Lieutenant Colonel Henry Lee commanded the troops that attacked the stockade, and Lieutenant Colonel Campbell commanded the troops who assaulted the star redoubt. The attack on both enemy positions

---

[33] Dunkerly and Williams, *Old Ninety-Six: A History and Guide*, 36-37
[34] Ibid.
[35] Ibid., 37

occurred simultaneously and was proceeded by an intense artillery barrage that commenced at noon.[36]

Lieutenant Colonel Lee's troops successfully gained control of the stockade west of Ninety Six after nearly an hour of heavy fighting and waited to learn the outcome of the assault on the star redoubt.[37] Lieutenant Colonel Campbell planned to storm the redoubt with the troops of his 1st Virginia as well as troops from the 1st Maryland.[38] A forlorn hope of fifty men drawn from both regiments and commanded by Lieutenant Isaac Duval of Maryland and Lieutenant Samuel Seldon of Virginia, raced forward out of the third parallel and into the abatis and ditch in front of the star redoubt to lead the assault. Many of the men carried long poles with hooks to pull down the sandbags that Lieutenant Colonel Cruger's troops had stacked on top of the parapet to protect against Greene's riflemen on the tower. General Greene described what happened.

> *Never was greater bravery exhibited than by the parties led on by Duval and Selden, but they were not so successful. They entered the Enemys Ditch and made every exertion to get down the sand Bags, which from the depth of the Ditch, height of the parapet, and under a galling fire, was rendered very difficult.*[39]

---

[36] O'Kelley, 256
[37] Ibid.
[38] Conrad, ed., "General Greene to Samuel Huntington, President of the Continental Congress, June 20, 1781," *The Papers of General Nathanael Greene*, Vol. 8, 419-420
[39] Ibid.

While Campbell's forlorn hope struggled to climb the steep embankment to get at the sandbags, they were stunned to find enemy troops in the ditch with them. Two enemy detachments had entered the ditch from the rear of the redoubt and circled around in opposite directions to slam into the flanks of the American troops. Both Lieutenant Duval and Lieutenant Seldon were wounded, and the fierce hand to hand struggle in the ditch and on the embankment cost numerous lives on both sides.

General Greene, *"Finding the Enemy defended their Works with great obstinacy and seeing but little prospect of succeeding without a heavy loss, and the issue doubtful...ordered the attack to be pushed no further.*[40] Greene added,

> *The behaviour of the Troops on this occasion deserves the highest commendations, both the Officers that entered the Ditch were wounded, and the greater part of their Men were either killed or wounded.*[41]

General Greene added praise for both his own troops and their adversaries in the three week siege.

> *The Troops have undergone incredible hardships during the Siege, and tho' the issue was not successful I hope their exertions will merit the approbation of Congress....The Siege has been*

---

[40] Conrad, ed., "General Greene to Samuel Huntington, President of the Continental Congress, June 20, 1781,"*The Papers of General Nathanael Greene*, Vol. 8, 419-420
[41] Ibid.

> *bloody on both sides from the frequent sallies that the Enemy made. The Garrison behaved with great spirit, and defended themselves with judgement and address.*[42]

General Greene estimated his losses in the attack in killed, and wounded at upwards of 40 men, principally at the star fort.[43] Losses for the entire siege were almost 150 men with more than 60% of them coming from the Virginia continentals.[44] British losses were reportedly less than 100 men for the siege.[45]

With approximately 2,000 enemy troops under Lord Rawdon reportedly bearing down on Ninety Six to relieve the garrison, General Greene had no choice but to lift the siege and withdraw north. After weeks of grueling fatigue duty and combat, Greene's troops were thoroughly demoralized by the turn of events. Lieutenant Colonel Henry Lee recalled that, "*gloom and silence pervaded the American camp; every one disappointed – every one mortified.*"[46]

Lord Rawdon reached Ninety Six on June 21st, two days after Greene's departure. Despite a shortage of provisions for his exhausted troops, many of who were unaccustomed to the summer heat of South Carolina and who suffered greatly for it, Rawdon pressed on after Greene with those of his troops still able to march. The pursuit was short lived, however, and

---

[42] Conrad, ed., "General Greene to Samuel Huntington, President of the Continental Congress, June 20, 1781,"*The Papers of General Nathanael Greene*, Vol. 8, 419-420
[43] Ibid, 421
[44] "Return of the Killed, Wounded, & Missing during the Siege of Ninety-Six," *Papers of the Continental Congress*, Vol. 2, Item 155, 165
[45] O'Kelley, 248
[46] Lee, 377

although Rawdon's vanguard caught up to Greene's rearguard, a river separated the two forces. With an alarming number of his men falling out of the ranks due to the heat, Lord Rawdon decided to end his pursuit and return to Ninety Six.

It was decided to abandon the isolated post at Ninety Six and march the garrison, joined by scores of loyalist refugees, back to Charleston. Lieutenant Colonel Cruger took on that responsibility while Lord Rawdon led 850 men eastward towards the Congaree River.[47]

When General Greene learned of these developments he redirected his march southward in an effort to catch Rawdon while his army was split. Both forces closed in on Orangeburg, where Rawdon joined a newly arrived British regiment of regulars and took up a strong defensive position. General Greene briefly considered an attack, but decided against it and withdrew his army instead to the High Hills of the Santee to rest and recover.[48] Lieutenant Colonel Lee explained why Greene's decision was necessary.

> *We had often experienced in the course of the campaign want of food, and had sometimes seriously suffered from the scantiness of our supplies, rendered more pinching by their quality; but never did we suffer so severely as during the few days' halt* [near Orangeburg]. *Rice furnished our substitute for bread, which, although tolerably relished by those familiarized to it from*

---

[47] C. Stedman, *The History of the Origin, Progress, and Termination of the American War*, Vol. 2, (London, 1794), 374

[48] Dennis M. Conrad, ed., "General Greene to Governor Thomas Burke of North Carolina, July 16, 1781,"*The Papers of General Nathanael Greene*, Vol. 9, (Chapel Hill, NC: University of North Carolina Press, 1997), 18-20

> *infancy, was very disagreeable to Marylanders and Virginians, who had grown up in the use of corn or wheat bread. Of meat we had literally none; for the few meager cattle brought to camp as beef would not afford more than one or two ounces per man. Frogs abounded in some neighboring ponds, and on them chiefly did the light troops subsist. They became in great demand from their nutritiousness; and, after conquering the existing prejudice, were diligently sought after. Even the alligator was used by a few.... The heat of the season had become oppressive, and the troops began to experience its effects in sickness.*[49]

General Greene agreed with Colonel Lee's assessment, informing the governor of North Carolina upon his arrival in the High Hills that, *"The Army has suffered incredible hardships; and requires a little relaxation."*[50]

Although General Greene wanted his troops to rest and restore themselves, he insisted that military discipline and order be maintained. Tents were *"regularly pitched"* and *"cleanliness"* preserved, while the roll was to be taken four times a day and company and battalion drill conducted daily.[51]

On July 19th, General Greene ordered Captain Thomas Edmunds to assume command of Richard Campbell's 1st Virginia Regiment.[52] A month earlier, Greene had ordered

---

[49] Lee, 386-387
[50] Conrad, ed., "General Greene to Governor Thomas Burke of North Carolina, July 16, 1781,"*The Papers of General Nathanael Greene*, Vol. 9, 20
[51] Conrad, ed., "General Greene's Orders, July 17, 1781,"*The Papers of General Nathanael Greene*, Vol. 9, 22
[52] Conrad, ed., "General Greene's Orders, July 19, 1781,"*The Papers of General Nathanael Greene*, Vol. 9, 43

Major Smith Snead of the 1st Virginia to take command of the 2nd Virginia Regiment in place of Lieutenant Colonel Hawes, whose ill health required his return to Virginia.[53]

As the ranking Virginian officer in Greene's army, Lieutenant Colonel Campbell assumed command of the Virginia brigade (both the 1st and 2nd Virginia Regiments) replacing General Isaac Huger, who was absent from the army. About a week later, a troop return for the army recorded approximately 1,200 men fit for duty, including 350 recently arrived North Carolina continentals.[54] Lieutenant Colonel Campbell's brigade of Virginians also accounted for about 350 troops.[55]

Greene estimated to General Washington in early August that the British had 4,000 regular troops and 400 cavalry as well as 1,000 Tory militia in South Carolina.[56] Greene optimistically reported that the continental soldiers, *"will amount to little more than 1500 men."*[57] Another 400 to 500 South Carolina state troops and 1500 to 2000 militia might be raised, wrote Greene, but the total would be far short of the 10,000 troops Greene believed necessary to take Charleston back from the British.[58]

---

[53] "June 19, 1781," *Orderly Book of Nathanael Greene, April 1– July 25, 1781*, (Huntington Library).

[54] Conrad, ed., "General Greene to George Washington, Footnote 3," *The Papers of General Nathanael Greene*, Vol. 9, 98

[55] Robert M. Dunkerly and Irene B. Boland, *Eutaw Springs: The Final Battle of the American Revolution's Southern Campaign*, (University of South Carolina Press, 2017), 112

[56] Conrad, ed., "General Greene to George Washington, August 6, 1781,"*The Papers of General Nathanael Greene*, Vol. 9, 139-140

[57] Conrad, ed., "General Greene to George Washington, August 6, 1781,"*The Papers of General Nathanael Greene*, Vol. 9, 140

[58] Ibid.

Although regaining Charleston was out of reach, General Greene hoped to strike at the British outside of Charleston and informed General Washington that once an adequate number of militia joined him, he intended to move against the British on the Congaree River.[59]

Lieutenant Colonel Alexander Stewart had assumed command of the detachment of British troops on the Congaree River at McCord's Ferry (upon the departure of Lord Rawdon who left South Carolina to restore his health). General Greene waited for most of August in the High Hills for sufficient militia to reinforce his army and although few arrived, he broke camp on August 24th, to confront Lieutenant Colonel Stewart. Greene declared to Lieutenant Colonel Henry Lee that, *"Reinforcements have been wanting nor are they by any means in that forwardness I could wish but we will make the most of them."*[60]

Lieutenant Colonel Campbell and his brigade of Virginia continentals marched north with the rest of Greene's army, away from McCord's Ferry. It was necessary to do so because the swamps and low ground to the south of the High Hills was flooded by recent heavy rains and the only way for the American army to cross the several rivers necessary to reach McCord's Ferry was to march north to Camden and then southwest to Howell's Ferry.[61]

Lieutenant Colonel Stewart learned of General Greene's movement well before Greene reached Howell's Ferry and

---

[59] Conrad, ed., "General Greene to George Washington, August 7, 1781,"*The Papers of General Nathanael Greene*, Vol. 9, 146-147

[60] Conrad, ed., "General Greene to George Washington, August 7, 1781,"*The Papers of General Nathanael Greene*, Vol. 9, 222-223

[61] Dunkerly and Boland, *Eutaw Springs: The Final Battle of the American Revolution's Southern Campaign*, 23-24

moved his force south to Eutaw Spring on August 27th. This brought him closer to Charleston and the supplies and reinforcements he expected any day.[62] The American army reached the former British camp at McCord's Ferry on September 2nd, where they were finally joined by hundreds of militia.[63] Greene moved further south and arrived at Burdell's Plantation, just seven miles northwest of Eutaw Springs on September 7th.[64]

Battle of Eutaw Springs

General Greene's army was on the march by 4:00 a.m. the following day. Lieutenant Colonel Stewart also sent men out from his camp at Eutaw Springs early on the morning of September 8th. Approximately 300 troops marched west several miles to forage for the army.[65] In their quest for sweet potatoes, they turned off the main road onto a plantation and General Greene's army marched right past them.[66]

Fortunately for the British, two American deserters informed Lieutenant Colonel Stewart that Greene's army was near. He sent out a second party of 140 infantry with 50 dragoons to investigate and they made contact with Greene's advance guard about three miles west of Eutaw Springs.[67]

The sharp, running skirmish that ensued attracted both the attention of the British foraging party, whose curiosity

---

[62] Dunkerly and Boland, *Eutaw Springs: The Final Battle of the American Revolution's Southern Campaign*, 24-25
[63] Ibid., 25
[64] Ibid., 33
[65] Ibid., 34
[66] Ibid., 34-35
[67] Ibid., 35

revealed their presence to the Americans and resulted in the capture of over half the party, as well as Lieutenant Colonel Stewart and his troops back at Eutaw Springs.[68]

General Greene ordered his militia, some 1,400 strong, to form for battle and they swept forward, Greene's advance units posting on the flanks of the militia line.[69] Behind the militia line trailed Greene's continentals. The Maryland brigade, some 400 strong, was posted on the left of the second line.[70] Lieutenant Colonel Campbell's Virginia brigade, 350 strong, held the center of the line and the North Carolina brigade, also 350 strong, held the right side of the line.[71] General Greene kept Lieutenant Colonel William Washington's continental cavalry and Captain Robert Kirkwood's Delaware continentals behind his second line in reserve.[72] Two 3 pound cannon advanced with the militia line and two 6 pound cannon advanced with the continental line.[73] Greene's force numbered approximately 2,000 men and they closed in on an enemy force that consisted of about half of that (after the loss of most of the foraging party).[74]

---

[68] Dunkerly and Boland, *Eutaw Springs: The Final Battle of the American Revolution's Southern Campaign*, 36

[69] Dunkerly and Boland, *Eutaw Springs: The Final Battle of the American Revolution's Southern Campaign*, 112, and Conrad, ed., "General Greene to Thomas McKean, President of the Continental Congress, September 11, 1781,"*The Papers of General Nathanael Greene*, Vol. 9, 328-329

[70] Dunkerly and Boland, *Eutaw Springs: The Final Battle of the American Revolution's Southern Campaign*, 112,

[71] Ibid.

[72] Conrad, ed., "General Greene to Thomas McKean, President of the Continental Congress, September 11, 1781,"*The Papers of General Nathanael Greene*, Vol. 9, 329

[73] Ibid.

[74] Dunkerly and Boland, *Eutaw Springs: The Final Battle of the American Revolution's Southern Campaign*, 112-113

Lieutenant Colonel Stewart may have been outnumbered, but many of the men with him at Eutaw Springs, both his regulars and militia, were seasoned veterans. Stewart formed his troops into one line, regular units posting on the flanks and Lieutenant Colonel Cruger's troops from Ninety Six holding the middle of the line.[75] They were deployed in wooded terrain a few hundred yards west of their camp, which was set up on open ground around a large brick house. Stewart placed loyalist riflemen in the house and issued orders to use the house as a fortified position if the enemy pushed the British back into their camp.[76]

General Greene, who ordered his army forward upon first contact with the enemy, described what happened as they closed in on the main British force.

> *The Militia were ordered to keep advancing as they fired. The Enemies advance parties were soon driven in, and a most tremendous fire began on both sides from right to left.... The Militia fought with a degree of spirit and firmness that reflects the highest honor upon this class of Soldiers.*[77]

The militia fought so well that Lieutenant Colonel Stewart was forced to deploy his reserve to bolster his line.[78]

---

[75] Dunkerly and Boland, *Eutaw Springs: The Final Battle of the American Revolution's Southern Campaign*, 38

[76] Ibid., 39-40

[77] Conrad, ed., "General Greene to Thomas McKean, President of the Continental Congress, September 11, 1781,"*The Papers of General Nathanael Greene*, Vol. 9, 329

[78] Dunkerly and Boland, *Eutaw Springs: The Final Battle of the American Revolution's Southern Campaign*, 50

Alas, Greene's militia began to waver and withdraw, so he ordered the North Carolina continentals under General Jethro Sumner to advance and support them. Despite their relative inexperience in the field, Greene reported that,

> [General Sumter's continentals *fought with a degree of obstinacy that would do honor to the best of veterans; and I could hardly tell which to admire most the gallantry of their Officers or the bravery of the Troops. They kept up a heavy and well directed fire, and the Enemy returned it with equal spirit...and great execution was done on both sides.*[79]

It was in the middle of this struggle, with the militia still withdrawing, that General Greene ordered Lieutenant Colonel Campbell's Virginian continentals and Colonel Otho Williams's Maryland continentals forward to join the fight. General Greene reported that

> *In this stage of the Action the Virginians under Lieut Col. Campbell, and the Maryland Troops under Col. Williams were led on to a brisk charge with trailed Arms, through a heavy cannonade, and a shower of Musquet Balls.*[80]

Greene proclaimed that

> *Nothing could exceed the gallantry and firmness of both Officers and Soldiers upon this occasion. They preserved their order, and pressed on with such*

---

[79] Conrad, ed., "General Greene to Thomas McKean, President of the Continental Congress, September 11, 1781,"*The Papers of General Nathanael Greene*, Vol. 9, 329
[80] Ibid., 329-331

unshaken resolution that they bore down all before them. The Enemy were routed in all quarters.[81]

Sadly, it was during this advance that Lieutenant Colonel Campbell, leading his Virginians on horseback, was struck by a musket ball in the chest. Lieutenant Colonel Henry Lee was with Campbell when he was shot and described the incident in his memoirs.

This excellent officer received a ball in his breast, in the decisive charge that broke the British line, while listening to [a question] *from Lieutenant-Colonel Lee....* [Campbell] *dropped on the pummel of his saddle speechless, and was borne to the rear by Lee's orderly dragoon.*[82]

In his report to Congress after the battle, General Greene confirmed that Lieutenant Colonel Campbell was struck down while leading his troops forward.[83]

Campbell's son, Archibald, who had risen to lieutenant in the 1st Virginia Regiment, was reportedly at his father's side when he was struck. Whether he assisted his father back to the rear or continued to fight with the rest of his regiment is unclear, but General Greene paid him a compliment after the

---

[81] Conrad, ed., "General Greene to Thomas McKean, President of the Continental Congress, September 11, 1781,"*The Papers of General Nathanael Greene*, Vol. 9, 331

[82] Lee, 472-473

[83] Conrad, ed., "General Greene to Thomas McKean, President of the Continental Congress, September 11, 1781,"*The Papers of General Nathanael Greene*, Vol. 9, 333

battle, referring to him as Lieutenant Campbell's, *"gallant son."*[84]

Accounts disagree on how long Campbell survived after he received his wound. Lieutenant Colonel Lee believe Campbell died, *"the moment he was taken from his horse,"* but a note in his memoirs from Lee's editor and son, Robert E. Lee, claimed that, *"Colonel Campbell, though in appearance dead, actually survived some hours after his fall, and on being told just before he expired that the Americans were victorious, exclaimed with the heroic fervor of Wolfe, 'Then I die contented.'"*[85]

The battle raged on and although General Greene's continentals fought well, Lieutenant Colonel Stewart's troops recovered from the shock of the American attack and rallied around the brick house, which was defended by a number of Stewart's troops. General Greene described what happened.

> *We kept close at the Enemy's heels after they broke, until we got into their Camp and a great number of Prisoners were continually falling into our hands, and some hundreds of the Fugitives run off towards Charles Town. But a party threw themselves into a large three story brick House which stands near the Spring, others took post in a picquetted Garden, while others were lodged in an impenetrable thicket.... Thus secured...the Enemy renewed the Action. Every exertion was made to dislodge them...[but] finding our Infantry galled by the fire of the Enemy, and our Ammunition mostly consumed, tho' both*

---

[84] Conrad, ed., "General Greene to Governor Thomas Nelson of Virginia, September 16, 1781,"*The Papers of General Nathanael Greene*, Vol. 9, 351

[85] Lee, 473

> *Officers and Men continued to exhibit uncommon acts of heroism, I thought proper to retire out of the fire of the House....*[86]

General Greene had lost yet another battle, but in doing so, his troops inflicted nearly 700 casualties on the British, 150 more than his own army suffered.[87]

Lieutenant Colonel Campbell was the highest ranking officer from either side to die at Eutaw Springs and General Greene lamented his loss, writing to Congress that,

> *Tho'* [Campbell] *fell with distinguished marks of honor, yet his loss is much to be regretted. He was the great Soldier and the firm patriot.*[88]

In a letter to Virginia's new governor, Thomas Nelson, a week after the battle, General Greene repeated his praise of Lieutenant Colonel Campbell, "*who was killed in the heat, and fury of the conflict,*" and who, "*bled more than once,*" for the American cause.[89] Greene added that Campbell deserved, "*all that can be said of a brave, active, and intrepid Soldier.*"[90]

---

[86] Conrad, ed., "General Greene to Thomas McKean, President of the Continental Congress, September 11, 1781,"*The Papers of General Nathanael Greene*, Vol. 9, 331-332

[87] Dunkerly and Boland, *Eutaw Springs: The Final Battle of the American Revolution's Southern Campaign*, 112-113

[88] Conrad, ed., "General Greene to Thomas McKean, President of the Continental Congress, September 11, 1781,"*The Papers of General Nathanael Greene*, Vol. 9, 333

[89] Conrad, ed., "General Greene to Thomas Nelson of Virginia, September 16, 1781,"*The Papers of General Nathanael Greene*, Vol. 9, 351

[90] Ibid.

Lieutenant Colonel Richard Campbell of Virginia lost his life in the service of his country in the Revolutionary War. He did not leave behind a detailed diary or a trove of letters from which to remember his life. Campbell's legacy was his service and ultimately, his sacrifice for the American cause of independence.

Campbell's nearly six years of service in the continental army included engagements in New Jersey and Pennsylvania as well as on the frontier and in the southern states of Georgia, North Carolina and South Carolina. A veteran of six major battles, (Brandywine, Germantown, Guilford Courthouse, Hobkirk Hill, Ninety-Six, and Eutaw Springs) and numerous smaller engagements on the frontier and in the South and mid-Atlantic, Campbell's service and sacrifice for his country is an accomplishment in its own right and a testament to his courage and patriotism. As such, he deserves to be remembered as General Nathanael Greene remembered him, as, **"*a brave, active, and intrepid Soldier.*"**

Battle of Eutaw Spring

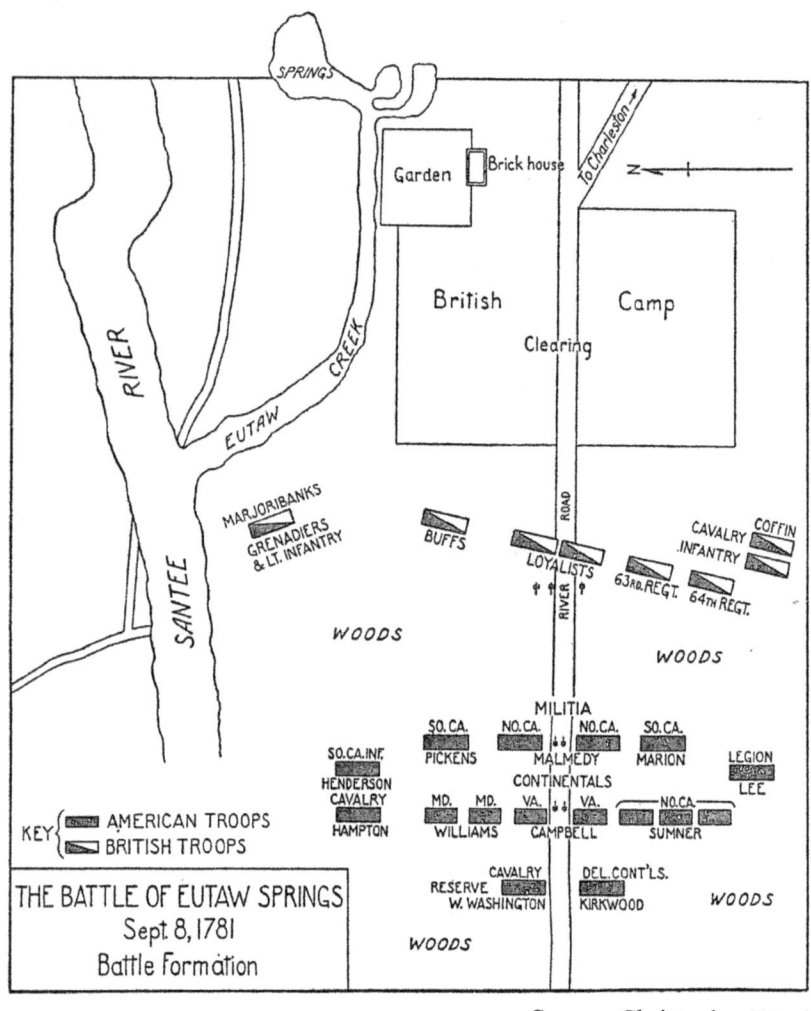

Source: Christopher Ward

Bibliography

Babits, Lawrence E. *A Devil of a Whipping: The Battle of Cowpens.* The University of North Carolina Press, 1998.

Babits, Lawrence E. and Joshua B. Howard, *Long, Obstinate, and Bloody: The Battle of Guilford* Courthouse, Chapel Hill, NC: The University of North Carolina Press, 2009.

Bearss, Edwin C. *The Battle of Sullivan's Island and the Capture of Fort Moultrie: A Documented Narrative and Troop Movement Maps.* U.S. Dept. of the Interior, 1968.

Borick, Carl P. *A Gallant Defense: The Siege of Charleston, 1780.* University of South Carolina Press, 2003.

Brumbaugh, Gaius M. "List of the Number of Persons in Dunmore County…Taken by Richard Campbell, November, 1775," *Revolutionary War Records,* Vol. 1. Washington, D.C., 1936.

Buchanan, John. *The Road to Guilford Courthouse: The American Revolution in the Carolinas.* John Wiley & Sons, 1997.

Cecere, Michael. *They Are Indeed a Very Useful Corps: American Riflemen in the Revolutionary War.* Heritage Books, 2006.

Cecere, Michael. *Wedded to My Sword: The Revolutionary War Service of Light Horse Harry Lee.* Heritage Books, 2012.

Dunkerly, Robert M. and Eric K. Williams, *Old Ninety-Six: A History and Guide,* Charleston, SC: A History Press, 2006.

Dunkerly, Robert M. and Irene B. Boland, *Eutaw Springs: The Final Battle of the American Revolution's Southern Campaign*, University of South Carolina Press, 2017.

Gilbreath, Amelia C. *Order Book, 1772-1774, Shenandoah County, VA*, Abstracted, 1986.

Hazard, Samuel ed., "Colonel Brodhead to Lieutenant Colonel Campbell, July 30th, 1779," *Pennsylvania Archives,* Series 1, Vol. 12, Philadelphia : Joseph Severns & Co., 1856.

Heitman, Francis B. *Historical Register of Officers of the Continental Army During the War of the Revolution, April 1775 to December 1783*. Washington, D.C., 1914.

Henings, William W. *The Statutes at Large; Being a Collection of all the Laws of Virginia,* Vol. 9, Richmond, 1821.

Idzerda, Stanley J., ed., *LaFayette in the Age of the American Revolution: Selected Letters and Papers*, Vol. 4, Ithaca and London: Cornell University Press, 1981.

Jackson, John W. *Valley Forge: Pinnacle of Courage*. Gettysburg, PA: Thomas Publications, 1992/

Kapp, Friedrich. *The Life of Frederich William von Steuben.* Corner House Publications, 1999.

Kellogg, Louise P. ed., *Frontier Advance on the Upper Ohio, 1778-79,* Madison, WI : Wisconsin Historical Society, 1916.

Lee Papers, Vol. 1-2. Collections of the New York Historical Society, 1871.

Lee, Robert E. ed., *The Revolutionary War Memoirs of General Henry Lee*, New York: Da Capo, 1998.

Lesser, Charles H. ed., "Monthly Return of the Forces in South Carolina, *The Sinews of Independence: Monthly Strength Reports of the Continental Army*, University of Chicago Press, 1976.

Lumpkin, Henry. *From Savannah to Yorktown: The American Revolution in the South.* toExcel Press, 1987.

Martin, Joseph Plum. *Private Yankee Doolittle: Being a Narrative of Some of the Adventures, Dangers and Sufferings of a Revolutionary Soldier*, Eastern Acorn Press, 1998, 73.   Originally published in 1840.

McGuire, Thomas. *The Philadelphia Campaign: Brandywine and the Fall of Philadelphia,* Vol. 1, Stackpole Books, 2006.

McGuire, Thomas J. *The Philadelphia Campaign: Germantown and the Roads to Valley Forge,* Vol. 2, Stackpole Books, 2007.

McMichael, James. "October 4, 1777 entry, Diary of Lieutenant James McMichael, of the Pennsylvania Line, 1776-1778, *The Pennsylvania Magazine of History and Biography,* Vol. 16, No. 2.

Morgan, William J. ed., *Naval Documents of the American Revolution*, Vol. 5, Washington: 1970.

Muhlenberg, Henry A. *The Life of Major-General Peter Muhlenberg of the Revolutionary Army*, Philadelphia, Cary and Hart, 1849.

Murphy, Daniel. *William Washington, American Light Dragoon.* Westholme, 2014.

O' Kelly, Patrick *Nothing but Blood and Slaughter: The Revolutionary War in the Carolinas,* Vol. 2-3, Blue House Tavern Press, 2005.

Palmer, William P. ed., "Arrangement of the Virginia Line, 1781," *Calendar of Virginia State Papers*, Vol. 1, Richmond, 1875.

Piecuch, Jim and John Beakes, *"Cool Deliberate Courage": John Eager Howard in the American Revolution.* Charleston, SC: The Nautical and Aviation Publishing Co. of America, 2009.

Piecuch, Jim. *Blood Be Upon Your Head: Tarleton and the Myth of Buford's Massacre.* Southern Campaign of the American Revolution, 2010.

Prentice Guy and Wendy M. Nettles. *Ninety Six National Historic Site Archeological Overview and Assessment.* Southeast Archeological Center, 2003.

Stedman, C. *The History of the Origin, Progress, and Termination of the American War*, Vol. 2, London, 1794.

Tarleton, Banastre. *A History of the Campaigns of 1780-1781 in the Southern Provinces of North America.* NH: AYER Company, 1999.
Originally printed in 1787

Tarter, Brent, ed., "April 14, 1776" in "The Orderly Book of the Second Virginia Regiment," *The Virginia Magazine of History and Biography*, Vol. 85, Richmond : Virginia Historical Society, 1977.

Tussell Jr., John B. *Birthplace of an Army: A Study of the Valley Forge Encampment*. Pennsylvania Historical and Museum Commission, 1998.

Ward, Harry M. *Charles Scott and the Spirit of '76*. Charlottesville, VA: University Press of Virginia, 1988.

Williams, Glenn F. *Year of the Hangman: George Washington's Campaign Against the Iroquis*. Westholme, 2005.

Wright, Jr., Robert K. *The Continental Army*, Washington, D.C.: Center of Military History, U.S. Army, 1983.

Select Published Series

Journals of the Continental Congress

Ford, Worthington C. ed. *Journals of the Continental Congress: 1774-1789,* Vol. 7, 11 Washington, DC.: Government Printing Office, 1908

Papers of the Continental Congress

National Archives, "List of Commissioned Officers Killed, Wounded and Captured in the action before Camden, 25 April, 1781," *Papers of the Continental Congress,* Vol. 2, Roll # 175, 168a.

National Archives, "Field Return of Infantry serving in the Southern Army of the United States Commanded by the Honorable Major-General Greene accounting for the killed etc. in the action of the 25th Instant," *Papers of the Continental Congress*, Vol. 2.

National Archives, "Return of the Killed, Wounded, & Missing during the Siege of Ninety-Six," *Papers of the Continental Congress*, Vol. 2, Item 155.

Papers of General Nathanael Greene

Showman, Richard K., ed., *The Papers of General Nathanael Greene*, Vol. 7, Chapel Hill, NC: The University of North Carolina Press, 1994.

Conrad, Dennis M. ed., *The Papers of General Nathanael Greene*, Vol. 8-9, Chapel Hill, NC: University of North Carolina Press,1995, 1997.

Papers of Thomas Jefferson

Boyd, Julian P. ed., *The Papers of Thomas Jefferson*, Vol. 4-5, Princeton, NJ: Princeton University Press, 1951-52.

Papers of George Washington: Revolutionary War Series

Grizzard, Frank E.ed., *The Papers of George Washington,* Vol. 8, Charlottesville: University Press of Virginia, 1998.

Chase, Philander D. ed. Vol. 9, Charlottesville: University Press of Virginia, 1999.

Grizzard, Frank E. ed., *The Papers of George Washington*, Vol. 10, Charlottesville: University Press of Virginia, 2000.

Chase, Philander D. Chase and Edward G. Lengel, eds., Vol. 11, Charlottesville: University Press of Virginia, 2001.

Grizzard, Jr., Frank E. ed., *The Papers of George Washington, Revolutionary War Series,* Vol. 12, University Press of Virginia, 2002.

Lengel, Edward G. ed., *The Papers of George Washington*, Vol. 13, Charlottesville: University of Virginia Press, 2003.

Hoth, David R. ed., *The Papers of George Washington*, Vol. 14, Charlottesville: The University of Virginia Press, 2004.

Lengel, Edward G. ed., *The Papers of George Washington,* Vol. 15, Charlottesville: University Press of Virginia, 2006.

Chase, Philander D., and William M. Ferraro, eds., *The Papers of George Washington,* Vol. 19, Charlottesville: University Press of Virginia, 2009.

Lengel, Edward G. ed., *The Papers of George Washington*, Vol. 20, Charlottesville : University of Virginia Press, 2010.

Ferraro, William M. ed., *The Papers of George Washington*, Vol. 21, Charlottesville : University of Virginia Press, 2012.

Huggins, Benjamin, ed., *The Papers of George Washington*, Vol. 22, Charlottesville : University of Virginia Press, 2013.

Ferraro, William M., ed., *The Papers of George Washington*, Vol. 23, Charlottesville : University of Virginia Press, 2015.

Writings of George Washington

Fitzpatrick, John C. ed. *Writings of George Washington,* Vol. 19. Washington, DC: U.S. Govt. Printing Officer, 1937.

Revolutionary Virginia: Road to Independence

Schreeven, William J. Van. and Robert L. Scribner, eds., *Revolutionary Virginia : The Road to Independence*, Vol. 2, University Press of Virginia, 1975.

Scribner, Robert L. and Brent Tarter, eds., *Revolutionary Virginia: The Road to Independence*, Vol. 5, University Press of Virginia, 1979.

Scribner, Robert L. and Brent Tarter, eds., *Revolutionary Virginia: The Road to Independence*, Vol. 6, Univ. Press of Virginia, 1981.

Tarter, Brent. ed., *Revolutionary Virginia: The Road to Independence,* Vol. 7, Part One, University Press of Virginia, 1983.

Unpublished Sources

McAlister, Val. *The Campbell's*: *Genealogy and History*, (unpublished).

Orderly Book of Nathanael Greene, April 1 – July 25, 1781, Huntington Library.

Steuben Papers (Microfilm) Rockefeller Library, Colonial Williamsburg Foundation, Williamsburg, Virginia.

Index

1st British Light Battalion, 42
1st Maryland Regiment, 82, 85, 91, 94, 107
1st Virginia Regiment, 22, 88-89, 103, 107, 112, 119
2nd Maryland Regiment, 82, 84-85, 91, 93
2nd Virginia Regiment, 20, 22, 88, 112
4th Virginia Convention, 3
4th Virginia Regiment, 22, 74
5th Virginia Convention, 13
5th Virginia Regiment, 23
6th Virginia Regiment, 52-53, 75
8th Pennsylvania Regiment, 52-53
8th Virginia Regiment, 2-4, 6-7, 9-12, 14, 16-17, 19-23, 25-27, 29, 31, 38
9th Virginia Regiment, 42-43, 64, 67. 69. 72-74
11th Virginia Regiment, 72, 75
12th Virginia Regiment, 22
13th Virginia Regiment, 21, 35, 37-38, 42, 44-45, 47-52, 54-56, 61, 64, 69
33rd British Regiment, 84
40th British Regiment, 40-41
60th British Regiment, 3

A

Alexander, Gen. William (Lord Stirling), 27-30
Augusta, GA, 100
Augusta Co., VA, 3

B

Beckford Parish, VA, 3
Birmingham Meeting House, PA, 28
Bowman, Col. Abraham, 20
Brandywine, Battle of, 26-32
British Guards, 84

Brodhead, Col. Daniel, 61, 63-69, 74
Buffalo Creek, NC, 78
Buford, Col. Abraham, 71
Burdell's Plantation, 114-115
Burnet, Maj. Ichadod, 78

C

Camden, SC, 90-91
   battle of, 92
   evacuated, 1781, 99
Campbell, Archibald, 89 119
Campbell, Rebecca, 1
Campbell, Richard,
   Pre-War, 1-2
   Capt. of 8th VA Regt., 2-6, 9, 11
   Maj. of 8th VA Regt., 14-17
   Rank Dispute, 19-21
   Transferred to 13th VA Regiment, 21-23, 35
   Sent back to Virginia, 24-25
   Returns to Army 25-26
   at Brandywine, battle of 27-29, 31
   with 13th Virginia Regt. 38
   at Germantown, battle of, 42, 44-45
   at Valley Forge, 47-52
   sent to Ft. Pitt, 54-56
   promoted to Lt. Col., 56
   at Ft. Pitt, 57, 61, 63, 67-70
   commands at Ft. McIntosh, 58-60
   13th Regiment re-designated 9th Virginia, 64
   commands at Ft. Laurens, 64-65
   dispute with Col. Brodhead, 65-66
   desire to leave frontier, 71
   transfers to 11th Virginia Regiment, 72, 75
   returns to Virginia, 1780, 73
   presides on court martial, 74
   returns to Ft. Pitt, 74
   commands southern detachment, 76-78
   joins Gen. Greene's army, 79

    at Guilford Courthouse battle of, 80, 82-85
        assumes command of 1st Virginia Regiment, 86-87
        writes to Gov. Jefferson, 89
        at Hobkirk's Hill, battle of, 91, 93, 95-96
            wounded at, 95
        at Siege of Ninety-Six, 100, 103-104, 107-108
        commands Virginia Brigade, 112-114
        at Eutaw Springs, battle of, 116, 118-122
            mortally wounded, 119-120
            death lamented, 121-122

Cape Fear, NC, 7-8
Caswell, Gen. Richard, 79
Charleston, SC, 9-10, 16, 99, 105, 110, 113-114
    battle of 1776, 10-13
    siege of 1780, 70-71
Chester, PA, 31, 38
Chesterfield, County Courthouse, 72, 74, 88
Chew, Benjamin, 40
Clark, George Rogers, 63
Clinton, Gen. Henry, 10-11, 70
Continental Congress, 6, 16, 19-20, 23, 33-34, 49-50, 55-57, 63, 69, 81, 97, 100, 105, 109, 119
Cornwallis, Gen. Charles, 8, 10, 76-77, 80-83, 85-86, 98
Cooches Bridge, DE, 26
Cowpens, Battle of, 76
Cross Creek, NC, 86
Cruger, Lt. Col., John, 101-102, 104, 107, 110, 116
Cumberland County, VA, 22

D

Davis, Col. William, 88
Delaware Continentals, 82, 92
Detroit, MI, 57, 68

Dilworth, PA, 28, 32
Dunmore Co. VA, 1-4
Dunmore Co. Committee, 1-2
Dunmore, Gov. John Murray, Earl of, 5-6

E

East Florida, 14-15
Edmonds, Capt. Thomas, 89-90, 112
Eutaw Springs, SC, 114
Eutaw Springs, Battle of 115-121

F

Fincastle, VA, 18
Fitzgerald, Col. John, 25
Ford, Lt. Col. Benjamin, 91, 93
French Alliance, 51

G

Gates, Gen. Horatio, 50, 72, 92
Germantown, battle of, 38-45
Gibson, Lt. Col., George, 37, 48, 52-53, 61-62
Granby, Fort, 100
Grayson, Col. William, 22
Great Bridge, VA, 5
Great Bridge, battle of, 5
Green, Col. John, 75, 79-80, 82-83, 85, 87-89
Greene, Gen. Nathanael,
  at Brandywine, 27, 31
  commands southern army, 74-79
  at Guilford, Courthouse, battle of, 80-86
  marches to South Carolina, 87-91
  at Hobkirk's Hill battle of, 92-96
  camps at Rugley's Mill, 97-99
  at siege of Ninety-Six, 100-110
  camps at the High Hills of the Santee, 111-113
  re-organizes Virginia Brigade, 112
  at Eutaw Springs battle of, 114-121
  laments Campbell's death, 121-122

Guilford Courthouse, battle of, 79-86
Gunby, Lt. Col., Benjamin, 91, 93-94

H

Haddrell's Point, SC, 10
Halifax, NC, 7
Hamilton, Gov. Henry, 63
Harrison, Capt., 65
Harrison, Col., 94
Hawes, Lt. Col., Samuel, 75, 79-80, 82, 88, 91, 93, 95-96, 103, 112
Head of Elk, MD, 26
Helpestine, Maj. Peter, 14
High Hills of the Santee, SC, 111-112, 114
High Rock, NC, 78
Higgins, Capt., 24
Hillsborough, NC, 76-78
Hobkirk's Hill, battle of, 91-96
Howe, Gen. William, 13, 23-26, 28, 31-33, 38, 40, 45-47
Howell's Ferry, SC, 114
Huger, Gen. Isaac, 79, 82, 88, 93, 103, 112

I

Iroquis, 64

J

Jefferson, Thomas, 73-74, 89
Johnson, George, 19

K

Kasciuszko, Col. Thaddeus, 103-104, 106
Kirkwood, Capt., Robert, 92, 116
Knox, Gen. Henry, 41
Knox, Capt. James, 18

L

Lancaster, PA, 32
Laurens, Henry, 49, 52, 56
Laurens, Ft. OH, 61-66
Lee, Gen. Charles, 7-9, 12-16
Lee, Maj. Henry, 81, 98-101, 107, 110-112, 114, 119-121
Lee, Robert E., 120
Lincoln, Gen. Benjamin, 70

Long Island, battle of, 28
Long Island, SC, 10-11
Luzerne, Chevalier de La, 96-97

M

Marion, Gen. Francis, 99-100
Markham, Maj., John, 20
Martin, Joseph Plub, 42
Maxwell, Gen. William, 27-28, 46
McCord's Ferry, SC, 113-114
McDougall, Gen. Alexander, 39
McIntosh, Ft., OH, 58-61, 68
McIntosh, Gen. Lachlan, 53-63
McMichael, Lt., James, 45
Mingoes, 64
Monmouth, battle of, 172-178
Monmouth Courthouse, NJ, battle of, 63, 70
Montresor, Capt., John, 21
Morgan, Daniel, Col., 18, 23, 49

Gen., 76, 82
Mott, Ft., 99-100
Moultrie, Col., William, 11-13
Muhlenberg, Peter
  Col., 2-4, 13-14, 16-17, 19
  Gen., 27, 38-39, 42, 45, 71-73
Musgrave, Col., Thomas, 40

N

Nash, Gen. Francis, 90
Nelson, Jr., Thomas, 121
Nevell, Col., John, 75
New Brunswick, NJ, 23-24
New Garden Meeting House, 81
New York, NY, 13, 70
Ninety-Six, SC, 116
  siege of, 100-110
Norfolk, VA, 5
Norfolk County, VA, 5-6

O

O'Hara, Gen. Charles, 84
Ohio Co., VA, 37
Orangeburg, SC, 99, 110-

111
Osborne Hill, PA, 28

P

Parker, Commodore, Peter, 11-13
Patton, Col. John, 22
Pennibacker's Mill, PA, 44
Perth Amboy, NJ, 24
Petersburg, VA, 220-221, 223-225
Philadelphia, PA, 21, 23, 25, 27, 31-32, 34, 38-39, 43, 45, 47, 70
Pickens, Gen., Andrew, 100, 107
Pitt, Fort, PA, 37-38, 48-50, 52, 56-58, 61, 64, 66, 69, 71-73
Portsmouth, VA, 5, 7
Pottsgrove, PA, 33
Powles Hook, battle of, 70
Princess Anne, Co., VA, 5-6

R

Race to the Dan, 76
Ramsey's Mill, SC, 90
Rawdon, Lord Francis, 90-95, 98-99, 110, 113
Reading, PA, 32-34
Ridley, Maj. Thomas, 103
Rugley's Mill, SC, 97
Russell, Col., William, 37, 44, 48, 50, 52-53

S

Saratoga, battle of, 18, 46
Savannah, GA, 15
Scott, Gen. Charles, 22-24, 29-30
Seldon, Lt. Samuel, 107-108
Shenandoah, Co., VA, 1
Smithfield, VA, 6
Snead, Maj. Smith, 103, 112
Stephen, Gen. Adam, 27-31, 41, 44, 46
St. Augustine, FL, 14
Staten Island, NY, 24
Steel, Col. Archibald, 59
Steuben, Gen. Freidrich von, 73-75
Stevens, Col. Edward, 79
Stewart, Lt. Col., Alexander, 113-115, 117, 120
Stony Point, battle of, 70

Suffolk, VA, 5-7
Sullivan, Gen. John, 27-30, 29-42, 46
Sullivan Island, SC, 10-13
Sumner, Gen. Jethro, 117-118
Sumter, Gen. Thomas, 99-100, 107
Sunbury, GA, 15

T

Tarleton, Lt. Col., Banastre, 81
Taylor, Richard, Maj., 67-68, 72-73, Lt. Col., 81
Taylor's Ferry, VA, 77-78
Trenton, NJ, 39

V

Valley Forge, PA, 32, 47-48, 50-52
Vernon, Maj. Frederick, 63
Vincennes, Battle of, 63
Virginia Committee of Safety, 6-7, 9

W

Watson, Col., John, 98
Watson, Ft. 100

Washington, Gen. George, 6, 18, 23-24, 37-38, 45-46, 62, 69, 70-71, 113
   view on Campbell's promotion, 19-21
   recalls Campbell to camp, 25-26
   at Brandywine, 26, 28, 31
   fall of Philadelphia, 32-34
   transfers Maj. Campbell to 13th Virginia Regt., 35
   at Germantown, 38-40, 43-44
   at Valley Forge, 47-49
   sends 13th Virginia Regt. to Ft. Pitt, 49-53
   transfers Lt. Col. Campbell to Western Dept., 55-56
   re-arranges army 1778, 63-64
   approves campaign against Indians 1779, 64-68
Washington, John

Augustine, 43
Washington, Lt. Col., William, 85, 92, 116
Waxhaws, battle of, 71
Wayne, Gen. Anthony, 27, 39, 41-42, 46
Webster, Col. James, 84
Weedon, Gen. George, 27, 39
West Augusta District, VA, 37
Whitemarsh, PA, 46
Williams, Col., Otho, 82, 93, 104, 118
Williamsburg, VA, 3, 6-7, 22

Wilmington, NC, 86, 98
Woodford,. Gen., William, 27, 29-30
Woodstock, VA, 1, 4, 24, 38, 73

Y

Yellow Springs, PA, 32
Yohogania Co., VA, 37
York, PA, 49-52

Heritage Books by Michael Cecere:

A Brave, Active, and Intrepid Soldier:
Lieutenant Colonel Richard Campbell
of the Virginia Continental Line

A Good and Valuable Officer:
Daniel Morgan in the Revolutionary War

A Universal Appearance of War:
The Revolutionary War in Virginia, 1775–1781

An Officer of Very Extraordinary Merit:
Charles Porterfield and the American War for Independence, 1775–1780

Captain Thomas Posey and the 7th Virginia Regiment

Cast Off the British Yoke:
The Old Dominion and American Independence, 1763–1776

Great Things are Expected from the Virginians:
Virginia in the American Revolution

He Fell a Cheerful Sacrifice to His Country's Glorious Cause:
General William Woodford of Virginia, Revolutionary War Patriot

In This Time of Extreme Danger:
Northern Virginia in the American Revolution

Second to No Man but the Commander in Chief:
Hugh Mercer, American Patriot

They Are Indeed a Very Useful Corps:
American Riflemen in the Revolutionary War

They Behaved Like Soldiers:
Captain John Chilton and the Third Virginia Regiment, 1775–1778

To Hazard Our Own Security:
Maine's Role in the American Revolution

Wedded to My Sword:
The Revolutionary War Service of Light Horse Harry Lee

www.ingramcontent.com/pod-product-compliance
Lightning Source LLC
Chambersburg PA
CBHW071726090426
42738CB00009B/1894